Easy Italian for English speakers

A guide to everyday Italian

A cura di Pauline Bell

AVALLARDI

Antonio Vallardi Editore s.r.l.
Corso Italia 13 - 20122 Milano

Copyright © 2000 Antonio Vallardi Editore

Ristampe: 9 8 7 6 5 4 3 2 1 0
           2004 2003 2002 2001 2000

ISBN 88-8211-504-6

SUMMARY

Part one

1. GUIDE TO PRONUNCIATION   9
A. The Italian alphabet
B. Pronunciation
C. Word stress

2. NUMBERS, WEIGHTS AND MEASURES   12
A. Cardinal numbers
B. Ordinal numbers
C. Weights
D. Measures

3. USEFUL VOCABULARY AND EXPRESSIONS   16
A. Parts of the day
B. Time
C. Days of the week
D. Months
E. Seasons
F. Holidays and festivities
G. Common expressions
H. Learning Italian

4. PERSONAL RELATIONS   21
A. Addressing people
B. Using titles and forms of address
C. Introducing yourself
D. Greeting people
E. Asking for information/help
F. Thanking people
G. Apologising
H. Sending greetings, congratulating and sympathising
I. At work

5. MEETING PEOPLE AND MAKING FRIENDS 28
A. Talking about the weather
B. Getting to know people
C. Talking about yourself
 • *Countries and nationalities*
D. Work
E. Religion
F. Likes and dislikes
G. Feelings

6. TRAVELLING 35
A. Asking for and giving directions
B. Public transport in the city
C. Travelling by car
D. By train
E. By air
F. Police and customs

7. EATING AND DRINKING 40
A. In the bar
B. At lunch/dinner
C. At the restaurant
D. Tastes and preferences

8. LOOKING FOR WORK 46
A. Getting the information you need
B. Giving information about yourself
C. Asking for details about work
D. Asking for clarification on pay

9. LOOKING FOR ACCOMODATION 50
A. Explaining what you want
B. Getting the information you need
C. Discussing the formalities

10. DOMESTIC PROBLEMS 54
A. Utilities
B. Problems and repairs
C. Getting on with your neighbours

11. SHOPPING AND SERVICES 58
A. Shopping for food and household goods
B. Department stores
C. Sundry
D. Payment

12. OFFICES AND BUREAUCRACY 64
A. Bureaucratic language
B. Information
C. At the post office
  • *Poste-office account*
  • *Registered letter with a return receipt*
D. At the bank
E. At the police headquarters/station

13. TAKING CARE OF YOUR HEALTH 72
  • *Health care*
A. Getting information and making an appointment
B. At the doctor's
C. At the dentist's/gynaecologist's/pediatrician's
D. At the chemist's
E. Emergencies

14. SCHOOL 79
A. Information and enrolments
B. In the classroom
C. School results

15. USING THE PHONE 82
  • *Emergency numbers and useful numbers*
A. Public phones
  • *Following the instructions for use*
B. Asking to speak to someone
C. Replying
D. Problems on the phone

16. READING AND UNDERSTANDING INSTRUCTIONS 87
A. Road signs
B. Signs and notices
C. Instructions for cashpoints
D. Electrical household appliances
E. Instructions for taking medicines

17. WRITING 91
A. Greetings cards
B. Postcards
C. Short messages
D. Writing letters
E. Curriculum vitae/CV
  • *Model CV*

18. CLASSIFIED ADVERTISEMENTS 99
A. Jobs
B. Property
C. Sundry

Part two

GRAMMAR

1. Sentence formation 107
A. Affirmative sentences
B. Interrogative sentences
C. Negative sentences

2. Gender forms 108

3. Articles 108
A. Definite article
B. Indefinite article
C. Quantifiers

4. Nouns and their plurals 110

5. Adjectives 111
A. Comparisons
B. Intensifying adjectives

6. Personal pronouns 113
A. Subject pronouns
B. Object pronouns

7. Possessive forms 114

8. Demonstrative 115

9. Indefinite adjectives and pronouns 115

10. Relative pronouns 116

11. Interrogatives 116
A. Interrogative adjectives
B. Interrogative pronouns
C. Other interrogative forms

12. Prepositions 117

13. Verbs 118
A. Auxiliary verbs
B. Regular verbs
C. Irregular verbs

PART ONE

1 GUIDE TO PRONUNCIATION

A. THE ITALIAN ALPHABET

The Italian alphabet contains **21 letters** (5 vowels/*vocali* **a**, **e**, **i**, **o**, **u** and 16 consonants /*consonanti*) and a further **5** letters of foreign origin – *j*, *k*, *w*, *x*, *y* – which can be found in words from other languages that are now in current usage.

For the letters of the Italian alphabet below, the pronunciation in brackets should be read as if it were English.

A	→	[ah]	**N**	→	[ennay]
B	→	[bee]	**O**	→	[oh]
C	→	[chee]	**P**	→	[pee]
D	→	[dee]	**Q**	→	[koo]
E	→	[ay]	**R**	→	[erray]
F	→	[effay]	**S**	→	[essay]
G	→	[gee]	**T**	→	[tee]
H	→	[ahkka]	**U**	→	[oo]
I	→	[ee]	**V**	→	[vee]
L	→	[ellay]	**Z**	→	[zeta]
M	→	[emmay]			

B. PRONUNCIATION

Rules

Italian pronunciation is not difficult if certain basic rules are followed:
• all letters, both vowels and consonants, must be pronounced with the exception of **h**;
• if 2 or 3 vowels follow each other in a word, each one is pronounced and retains its own individual sound: *dietro* → [dee-e-tro]

(behind); *suono* → [soo-<u>oh</u>-no] (sound); *aiuto* → [a-y<u>oo</u>-to] (help);
• If a word contains a double consonant (*ss*, *rr*) you hear – and pronounce – both consonants: *passo* → [p<u>a</u>sso] (step); *ombrello* → [ombr<u>e</u>llo] (umbrella).

Pronunciation of vowels

Be careful with the pronunciation of vowels:

a   is pronounced like [ah] in 'rather': *lana* → [l<u>ah</u>na] (wool) or like [a] in 'hat': *atto* → [<u>a</u>tto] (act);

e   is pronounced like [ay] in 'day': *sei* → [s<u>ay</u>] (six) or like [e] in 'egg': *spesso* → [sp<u>e</u>sso] (often);

i   is pronounced like the long English [ee] in 'sheep': *fila* → [f<u>ee</u>la] (queue, row) or like [i] as in 'dinner': *tribù* → [trib<u>oo</u>] (tribe);

o   can be pronounced [oh] as in 'phone': *nome* → [n<u>oh</u>may] (name) or [o] as in 'got'; *notte* → [n<u>o</u>ttay] (night);

u   is pronounced like [oo] in 'spoon': *luna* → [l<u>oo</u>na] (moon).

Pronunciation of consonants

Most consonants are pronounced as in English but be careful with the following:

c, cc   before **e**, **i** is pronounced as the English [ch] in 'cheese': *Cina* → [ch<u>ee</u>na] (China);

c   before **a**, **o**, **u** is pronounced as the English [k] in 'cat': *casa* → [k<u>ah</u>sa] (house);

ch   before **e**, **i** is the hard sound [k] as in 'car': *perché* → [perk<u>ay</u>] (why);

g, gg   before **e**, **i** is pronounced as the English [dg] in 'jam': *gente* → [dg<u>e</u>ntay] (people);

g   before **a**, **o**, **u** is pronounced as the English [g] in 'good': *gonna* → [g<u>oh</u>nna] (skirt);

gh   before **e**, **i** is pronounced as the English [g] in 'gate': *ghepardo* → [gep<u>ah</u>rdo] (cheetah);

gl   before **i** is pronounced like the [-lli] in 'brilliant': *figlio* → [f<u>ee</u>lyo] (son);

gn   is pronounced like the [-ni] in 'opinion': *campagna* → [kam-pahnya] (countryside);

gu   is pronounced as the English [gw] in 'Gwyneth': *guanti* → [gwahnti] (gloves);

h   is never pronounced, but it modifies **c** and **g** (see *ch* and *gh*): *hotel* → [otel] (hotel);

qu   is pronounced as the English [kw] in 'question': *quando* → [kwahndo] (when);

s   is generally pronounced soft like [s] in 'salt', but sometimes hard like [z] in 'zoo': *spalla* → [spahlla] (shoulder); *viso* → [veezo] (face);

sc   before **e**, **i** is pronounced [sh] as in 'shell': *uscita* → [oo-sheeta] (exit);

sch   before **e**, **i** is pronounced [sk] as in 'ski': *schermo* → [skermo] (screen);

z, zz   is generally pronounced soft [ts] as in 'bits', but sometimes hard [ds] as in 'roads': *grazie* → [grahtsiay] (thank you); *zero* → [dsero] (zero).

C. WORD STRESS

The main stress in Italian words is variable. Generally the vowel of the next-to-last syllable is stressed, but it can fall on the third or fourth from the last. When a final vowel is stressed, it has an accent written over it: *più* → [pioo] (more).

2 NUMBERS, WEIGHTS AND MEASURES

A. CARDINAL NUMBERS

0	zero/nought	zero
1	one	uno
2	two	due
3	three	tre
4	four	quattro
5	five	cinque
6	six	sei
7	seven	sette
8	eight	otto
9	nine	nove
10	ten	dieci
11	eleven	undici
12	twelve	dodici
13	thirteen	tredici
14	fourteen	quattordici
15	fifteen	quindici
16	sixteen	sedici
17	seventeen	diciassette
18	eighteen	diciotto
19	nineteen	diciannove
20	twenty	venti
21	twenty-one	ventuno
22	twenty-two	ventidue
23	twenty-three	ventitré
24	twenty-four	ventiquattro

25	twenty-five	**venticinque**
26	twenty-six	**ventisei**
27	twenty-seven	**ventisette**
28	twenty-eight	**ventotto**
29	twenty-nine	**ventinove**
30	thirty	**trenta**
31	thirty-one	**trentuno**
40	forty	**quaranta**
50	fifty	**cinquanta**
60	sixty	**sessanta**
70	seventy	**settanta**
80	eighty	**ottanta**
90	ninety	**novanta**
100	a hundred	**cento**
101	a hundred and one	**centouno**
200	two hundred	**duecento**
300	three hundred	**trecento**
400	four hundred	**quattrocento**
500	five hundred	**cinquecento**
600	six hundred	**seicento**
700	seven hundred	**settecento**
800	eight hundred	**ottocento**
900	nine hundred	**novecento**
1.000	a thousand	**mille**
10.000	ten thousand	**diecimila**
100.000	a hundred thousand	**centomila**
1.000.000	a million	**un milione**
1.000.000.000	a billion	**un miliardo**

B. ORDINAL NUMBERS

first	**primo**
second	**secondo**

third	terzo
fourth	quarto
fifth	quinto
sixth	sesto
seventh	settimo
eighth	ottavo
ninth	nono
tenth	decimo
eleventh	undicesimo
twelfth	dodicesimo
thirteenth	tredicesimo
fourteenth	quattordicesimo
fifteenth	quindicesimo
sixteenth	sedicesimo
seventeenth	diciassettesimo
eighteenth	diciottesimo
nineteenth	diciannovesimo
twentieth	ventesimo
thirtieth	trentesimo
hundredth	centesimo
thousandth	millesimo

C. WEIGHTS

gram	grammo
a hundred grams	etto(grammo)
kilo	chilo(grammo)
a hundred kilos	quintale
ton	tonnellata

In Italy there is no equivalent measure for "pound" and "half a pound". The *etto* (100 g) tends to be used for weights other than a kilo (*un kilo*) and half a kilo (*mezzo kilo*).

Vorrei 3 etti di funghi.   I'll have 300 g of mushrooms.

D. MEASURES

Length

millimetre	millimetro
centimetre	centimetro
decimetre	decimetro
metre	metro
kilometre	chilometro

Area

square metre	metro quadrato
hectare	ettaro
square kilometre	chilometro quadrato

Volume and capacity

litre	litro
hectolitre	ettolitro
cubic centimetre	centimetro cubo
cubic decimetre	decimetro cubo
cubic metre	metro cubo

3 USEFUL VOCABULARY AND EXPRESSIONS

A. PARTS OF THE DAY

morning	la mattina
afternoon	il pomeriggio
day	il giorno/la giornata
evening	la sera/la serata
this morning	stamattina
this afternoon	oggi pomeriggio
this evening	stasera
tonight	stanotte
by day	di giorno
in the evening	di sera
at night	di notte
at midday	a mezzogiorno
at midnight	a mezzanotte
at sunset	al tramonto

B. TIME

an hour	un'ora
half an hour	mezz'ora
quarter of an hour	un quarto d'ora
a minute	un minuto
a second	un secondo
(official) summer-time	l'ora legale

To talk about the 24-hour day the numbers from 1 to 12 are generally used. When you say *"Ci vediamo alle sei"*/"See you at six" you usually mean six in the evening! However, the 24-hour clock is used in newspapers and for timetables. *"Il treno parte alle 18.00"*/ "The train leaves at 18.00".

What time is it?	**Che ore sono?**
It's one o'clock.	**È l'una.**
It's two o'clock/ten past three/ quarter past four/half past six/ twenty-five to eight/twenty to eight/quarter to nine/ten to ten.	**Sono le due/le tre e dieci/le quattro e un quarto/ le sei e mezzo/le sette e trentacinque/le otto meno venti/le nove meno un quarto/le dieci meno dieci.**
It's midday/midnight.	**È mezzogiorno/mezzanotte.**
It's exactly eight (o'clock).	**Sono le otto in punto.**
What time should I come?	**A che ora devo venire?**
Come at two (o'clock).	**Venga alle due.**
The shop opens at nine/closes at seven.	**Il negozio apre alle nove/chiude alle sette.**
The 20.43 train for Bologna is leaving from platform 4.	**Il treno delle 20.43 per Bologna è in partenza dal binario 4.**

C. DAYS OF THE WEEK

Monday	**lunedì**	Friday	**venerdì**
Tuesday	**martedì**	Saturday	**sabato**
Wednesday	**mercoledì**	Sunday	**domenica**
Thursday	**giovedì**		

In Italian the days of the week are masculine (*il giovedì*) with the exception of Sunday which is feminine (*la domenica*). Adjectives will obviously need to agree as in the following examples:

I'll come again next Thursday.	**Tornerò giovedì prossimo.**
I'll come back next Sunday.	**Tornerò domenica prossima.**

D. MONTHS

January	gennaio	July	luglio
February	febbraio	August	agosto
March	marzo	September	settembre
April	aprile	October	ottobre
May	maggio	November	novembre
June	giugno	December	dicembre

E. SEASONS

Spring	Primavera	Autumn	Autunno
Summer	Estate	Winter	Inverno

In Italian, *primavera* and *estate* are feminine whereas *autunno* and *inverno* are masculine.

I went to the seaside last summer.	L'estate scorsa sono andato al mare.
I went to the mountains last winter.	L'inverno scorso sono andato in montagna.

F. HOLIDAYS AND FESTIVITIES

New Year's Day	Capodanno
Epiphany	Epifania
Carnival	Carnevale
Shrove Tuesday	Martedì grasso
Thursday/Saturday before Lent	Giovedì/sabato grasso
Ash Wednesday	Mercoledì delle Ceneri
Lent	Quaresima
Palm Sunday	Domenica delle Palme
Holy Week	Settimana Santa
Easter	Pasqua
Easter Monday	Lunedì dell'Angelo
Liberation Day	Liberazione (25 aprile)
Labour Day	Festa del lavoro (1° maggio)
Ascension (Day)	Ascensione

Pentecost	Pentecoste
Corpus Christi (Day)	Corpus Domini
All Saints' Day	Ognissanti
All Souls' Day	Giorno dei morti
Immaculate Conception (Day)	Immacolata Concezione
Advent	Avvento
Christmas Eve	Vigilia di Natale
Christmas (Day)	Natale
Boxing Day	Santo Stefano
Sunday(s)/public holiday(s)	giorno/i festivo/i
working day(s)	giorno/i feriale/i
public holiday/religious holiday	festa nazionale/festa religiosa

G. COMMON EXPRESSIONS

Yes.	Sì.
No.	No.
Please.	Per favore.
Thank you/Thanks.	Grazie!
You're welcome!	Prego!
Good! All right!	Bene! D'accordo!
Sorry!/Excuse me!	Scusi!
It doesn't matter!	Non importa!
Bless you!	Salute! (when someone sneezes)
Help!	Aiuto!
Could you help me?	Può aiutarmi?
Look out!	Attenzione!
May I?	Permette?
Excuse me!	Permesso! (to get past someone e.g. on crowded bus)
May I come in?	È permesso? (before entering someone's home)
Please (take a seat/sit down).	Prego (si accomodi)!

H. LEARNING ITALIAN

I'm a foreigner.	Sono straniero.
I come from outside the European community.	Sono extracomunitario.
Do you speak English?	Parla inglese?
I don't speak Italian.	Non parlo italiano.
I don't speak Italian very well.	Non parlo bene l'italiano.
I can speak only a little Italian.	Parlo solo un po' d'italiano.
I'm studying Italian.	Sto studiando l'italiano.
I'm doing an Italian course for foreigners.	Frequento un corso d'italiano per stranieri.
I don't understand.	Non capisco.
I haven't understood.	Non ho capito.
Sorry. What did you say?	Scusi, come ha detto?
Could you repeat that, please?	Può ripetere, per favore?
Could you speak more slowly, please?	Può parlare più lentamente, per favore?
Could you tell me what this (word) means?	Potrebbe spiegarmi questa parola?
What does… mean?	Che cosa vuol dire…?
How do you pronounce/ say this?	Come si pronuncia?/ Come si legge?
How do you say it in Italian?	Come si dice in italiano?
Could you spell it for me?	Può fare lo spelling?/ Come si scrive, lettera per lettera?
I can't write (any) Italian.	Non so scrivere in italiano.
Could you write the address, please?	Per favore, potrebbe scrivermi l'indirizzo?

4 PERSONAL RELATIONS

A. ADDRESSING PEOPLE

In Italian, the familiar **tu** form is used with family, friends, colleagues, anyone you know well, young people and children. Young people tend to use *tu* among themselves even if they don't know each other.

If you want to speak to someone you don't know or if you are in a work situation which requires polite dealings with people you would use the courtesy form **lei**, which is actually the feminine, third person singular form. N.B. Be careful with agreement; if your interlocutor is a man then adjectives and participles are masculine: "Have you been paid?"/"*Lei è stato pagato?*" (man) or "*Lei è stata pagata?*" (woman).

When speaking to more than one person, the second person plural form **voi** is used: "Have you been paid?"/"*Voi siete stati pagati?*". The use of the third person plural **loro** to express extreme courtesy has almost disappeared.

The familiar form *tu* / The polite form *lei*

What are you doing tomorrow?	**Che cosa fai domani?** (familiar) **Che cosa fa domani?** (polite)
I've brought you a present.	**Ti ho portato un regalo.** (familiar) **Le ho portato un regalo.** (polite)
Can/Could you pass me the calculator, please?	**Puoi passarmi la calcolatrice/ Mi passi la calcolatrice, per favore?** (familiar) **Può passarmi la calcolatrice/ Mi passa la calcolatrice, per favore?** (polite)

Are you enrolled on the course?	**Sei iscritto (man) / Sei iscritta (woman) a questo corso?** (familiar) **Lei è iscritto (man) / Lei è iscritta (woman) a questo corso?** (polite)

B. USING TITLES AND FORMS OF ADDRESS

• Unlike in many countries, in Italy men are often addressed using their qualification as a sort of title. For example, you will hear men referred to as *ingegnere* (engineer), ragioniere (accountant), geometra (surveyor), *avvocato* (lawyer) and above all **dottore** (**doctor**). These titles are used, at times indiscriminately, to make people feel important. As titles should be used only where appropriate, it's best not to imitate this habit. If the man you are speaking to is neither a doctor nor a lawyer, it is best simply to say **signore** (**Mr**) and to add his surname if you know it. Or simply don't use anything!

Good morning, Mr Rossi.	**Buongiorno, dottor Rossi.**
Good evening.	**Buonasera, ingegnere.**
How are you, Mr Galli?	**Come sta, signor Galli?**
Thank you, (Sir).	**Grazie, signore.**
Good-bye.	**Arrivederla.**

N.B. *Signore* and *dottore* are abbreviated to **signor** and **dottor** when followed by a surname or name (e.g. Mr Galli/*Signor Galli*).

• Generally, titles are not used as often with women. At work you will sometimes hear titles (especially **dottoressa** and **professoressa**) being used. Outside the work place, **signora** is used. The distinction between **signorina** (**Miss**) and **signora** (**Mrs**) is also less used nowadays. Whereas *signorina* used to be used for an unmarried woman regardless of her age, the tendency now is to use *signora* with all women over, say, 30 years of age.

Hello, Mrs Bianchi.	**Buongiorno, signora Bianchi.**
Thank you, (Madam).	**La ringrazio, signora.**
Good evening, (Mrs/Miss...).	**Buonasera, professoressa.**

Could you see/examine me, Doctor?	Dottoressa, può visitarmi?

C. INTRODUCING YOURSELF

Good morning. Fred Chandler.	Buongiorno. Fred Chandler.
David Saunders. How do you do.	David Saunders, piacere.
Jennifer Fisher.	Sono Jennifer Fisher.
I'm/My name's Elizabeth Brown.	Mi chiamo Elizabeth Brown.
Let me introduce myself. Mark Granger from Almex.	Posso presentarmi? Mark Granger della ditta Almex.
Pleased to meet you.	Molto lieto/Piacere di conoscerla/ Lieto di fare la sua conoscenza.
The pleasure is mine.	Il piacere è mio.
This is Joseph.	Questo è Joseph.
This is Mrs Linda Scott.	Ti presento la signora Linda Scott.
I'd like you to meet Doctor Robinson.	Vorrei presentarle il dottor Robinson.
What's your name?	Come ti chiami?/Come si chiama?
What's your name/surname?	Qual è il tuo nome/cognome?
You must be Mr…	Lei è il signor…?
Haven't we met before?	Ci siamo già visti?

D. GREETING PEOPLE

Ciao is the universally recognised Italian greeting. Be careful not to overuse it, however, as it should be reserved for people you are on familiar terms with (*tu*). *Ciao* is used both on meeting someone and on saying goodbye.

Salve is another form which is increasingly used by young and older people alike. It is polite but informal and friendly and so recommended for use with people you know fairly well.

Buongiorno is the correct form to use with people you address as *lei*.

Hello/Hi, Giorgio.	Ciao, Giorgio.
Well, I must be going. Bye!	Be', adesso devo andare. Ciao.
Hello/Hi, how are you/things?	Salve, come va?
Good morning.	Buongiorno.
Good morning, Mr Rossi.	Buongiorno dottor Rossi.
Good evening.	Buonasera.
Good night!	Buonanotte.
Good-bye!	Arrivederci.
Good-bye, Mr Neri.	Arrivederla signor Neri.
See you tomorrow.	A domani.
See you this evening.	A stasera.
See you soon.	A presto.
See you later.	A tra poco.
Good-bye!	Addio.
Hello, everybody.	Saluti a tutti.
Welcome to Italy!	Benvenuto/a in Italia!
See you (sometime)!	Ci vediamo.
See you/Hear from you soon!	Ci sentiamo presto.
How are you?	Come stai?/Come sta?
How are things?	Come va?
Good/Great, thanks. And you?	Bene/Benissimo, grazie. E tu?
Not so bad/Could be better, thanks. And you?	Abbastanza bene/ Non c'è male, grazie. E lei?
Not so good.	Non molto bene.

E. ASKING FOR INFORMATION/HELP

Could I have some information, please?	Può darmi un'informazione, per favore?
I'd like some information.	Vorrei/Mi servono delle informazioni.

Excuse me. Could you help me?	Scusi, può aiutarmi?
Would you mind helping me, please?	Le dispiacerebbe aiutarmi, per favore?
I need some help.	Ho bisogno di un aiuto.

F. THANKING PEOPLE

Thanks/Thanks a lot/Thank you very much.	Grazie/Molte grazie/Mille grazie.
You're welcome!/Not at all!/Don't mention it!	Prego/Di niente/Non c'è di che.
I can't thank you enough.	Non so come ringraziarla.
It's really kind of you.	È veramente gentile da parte sua.
Thanks. It was a nice thought.	Grazie del pensiero.
Thanks for the information.	Grazie dell'informazione.
Thanks for everything.	Grazie di tutto.
Thank you for (all) your help.	La ringrazio dell'aiuto.
It was nice of you to help me.	È stato gentile ad aiutarmi.
Don't mention it/No trouble at all.	S'immagini.

G. APOLOGISING

Sorry!	Scusa.
I'm sorry!	Scusi/Mi scusi.
I'm sorry to bother you/I'm late.	Scusi il disturbo/il ritardo.
I am sorry.	Mi dispiace.
I'm really sorry about the misunderstanding.	Sono molto spiacente di questo malinteso.
I'm terribly sorry. It's (all) my fault.	Sono desolata. È colpa mia.
Please accept my apologies.	Le faccio le mie scuse.

H. SENDING GREETINGS, CONGRATULATING AND SYMPATHISING

• Exchanging greetings in person or by writing cards is still very common in Italy. Remembering someone's birthday or anniversary in this way is considered to be a thoughtful gesture. The easiest and most common greeting is **Auguri**, which can be used on all official occasions like Christmas, New Year and Easter but also for individual greetings for important events such as birthdays, weddings or name-days. To send written greetings, see → **17. Writing**: A. Greetings cards.

Auguri!/Tanti auguri!	Best wishes!
Alla salute!/Cin cin!	(Your) Good health!/Cheers!
Buon Natale!	Merry Christmas!
Buon Anno!	Happy New Year!
Buone feste!	Happy Christmas!/New Year!/Easter! etc.
Buona Pasqua!	Happy Easter!
Buon compleanno!	Happy birthday!

• Different greetings exist for other circumstances (e.g. to wish someone good luck, to give encouragement etc.).

Auguri! Buon lavoro!	Have a good day!
Buon appetito!	Enjoy your meal!
Grazie, altrettanto!	Thanks. The same to you!
Buon viaggio!	Have a nice trip/journey!
Buone vacanze!/Buon fine settimana!	Have a good holiday!/Have a good weekend!
Buona fortuna!	Good luck!
Buon divertimento!	Enjoy yourself!
Buona giornata!/Buona serata!	Have a nice day/evening!
Complimenti!	Well done!
Congratulazioni!/Felicitazioni!	Congratulations!

• Good manners also dictate that a note expressing sympathy (*condoglianze*) should be sent upon someone's death.

With sympathy/I'm really sorry.	Condoglianze/Le faccio le mie condoglianze.
Please accept my deepest sympathy.	La prego di accettare le mie condoglianze.
I was really sorry to hear about your father's death.	Mi dispiace molto per la morte di suo padre.

I. AT WORK

The following are common phrases which may come in useful at work:

What would you like?	Desidera?/Che cosa desidera?
Can I help you?	Posso esserle d'aiuto?
Anything else?	Serve altro?
What will you have?	Che cosa prende?
What can I get you?	Che cosa posso servirle?
There you are, Sir.	Ecco a lei, signore.
What do I have to do?	Che cosa devo fare?
Where do I begin?	Da dove devo cominciare?
Where are the floor cloths/detergents…?	Dove posso trovare gli stracci/i detersivi…?
I need a sweeping brush/rope…	Mi servirebbe una scopa/una corda…
Is that all right?	Così va bene?

5 MEETING PEOPLE AND MAKING FRIENDS

A. TALKING ABOUT THE WEATHER

It's cold/hot.	**Fa freddo/Fa caldo.**
It's muggy.	**C'è afa.**
It's a nice/horrible day, today.	**Oggi il tempo è bello/brutto.**
What a lovely day!	**Che bella giornata!**
What horrible weather!	**Che tempo orribile!**
It's pouring down.	**Piove a dirotto.**
It's been raining.	**Ha piovuto.**
A storm is on the way.	**Sta per arrivare un temporale.**
It's thirty degrees in the shade.	**Ci sono trenta gradi all'ombra.**
Is it always this cold in Milano?	**Fa sempre così freddo qui a Milano?**
It's nice here.	**Si sta bene qui.**

B. GETTING TO KNOW PEOPLE

Examples using both *tu* and *lei* are given. See → **4. Personal Relations**: A. Addressing people.

What's your name?	**Come ti chiami/Come si chiama?**
How old are you?	**Quanti anni hai/ha?**
Where are you from?	**Da dove vieni?**
Are you Italian?	**Sei italiano/a?**
Where does he/she come from?	**Di che paese è?**
You speak Italian well!	**Parli bene l'italiano!**

Are you studying or working?	Studi o lavori?
Do you know anyone here in Bologna?	Conosce qualcuno qui a Bologna?
What's it like living here?	Come si vive in questa città?
Are you getting bored?	Ti stai annoiando?
Can I get you something (to drink)/a coffee/a soft drink/ an aperitif?	Posso offrirti qualcosa/ un caffè/una bibita/un aperitivo?
Can I take/walk you home?	Posso accompagnarti a casa?
Are you free this evening?	Sei libera stasera?
Where do you live?	Dove abiti?
What do you do?	Che lavoro fai?
Can I phone you tomorrow?	Posso telefonarle domani?
When shall we see each other?	Quando ci vediamo?
What shall we do?	Che cosa facciamo?
What are you doing this evening?	Che cosa fate questa sera?
Where are you meeting?	Dove vi date appuntamento?
We could go dancing.	Si potrebbe andare a ballare.
What about going to play tennis?	Che ne dici di (andare a) giocare a tennis?
Is there a swimming pool near here?	C'è una piscina da queste parti?
Would you like to go to the cinema?	Avresti voglia di venire al cinema?
What film is on this evening?	Che film danno stasera?
What time does the film start?	A che ora comincia il film?
Shall we have something to eat first?	Prima mangiamo qualcosa insieme?
Yes, all right/O.K.!	Sì, d'accordo/Va bene.
Gladly!/Willingly!	Con piacere/Volentieri.
I'm sorry. I can't.	Mi dispiace, non posso/ Mi rincresce, non sono libera.

| I'm sorry, but I have to go now. | Scusa, ma devo andare adesso. |
| Some other time. | Sarà per un'altra volta. |

C. TALKING ABOUT YOURSELF

I'm not Italian.	Non sono italiano.
I'm Canadian.	Sono canadese.
I was born in Toronto.	Sono nato a Toronto.
I'm 38.	Ho 38 anni.
I'm single (man)/single (woman)/ engaged.	Sono celibe/nubile/fidanzato/a.
I've been married for five years.	Sono sposato da cinque anni.
I've got two children.	Ho due bambini.
I haven't any relatives in Italy.	Non ho parenti in Italia.
I live alone here in Torino.	Sono solo qui a Torino.
I've got a younger brother/sister.	Ho un fratello/una sorella più giovane di me.
I'm the eldest of four children.	Sono il maggiore di quattro fratelli.
My family live in Scotland.	La mia famiglia vive in Scozia.
I've been in Italy for two months.	Sono in Italia da due mesi.
I live in Milano.	Vivo a Milano.
I live in Corso Garibaldi.	Abito in Corso Garibaldi.
I studied accountancy back home.	Al mio paese ho studiato da ragioniere.
I worked as a clerk in Aberdeen.	Ad Aberdeen lavoravo come impiegata.
I'm studying architecture at university.	Studio architettura all'università.
I'm in my fourth year of engineering.	Sono al quarto anno di ingegneria.
I'm looking for work.	Sto cercando un lavoro.

COUNTRIES AND NATIONALITIES

Some of the main English-speaking countries:

Australia/Australian	Australia/australiano/a
Canada/Canadian	Canada/canadese
England/English	Inghilterra/inglese
Finland/Finnish	Finlandia/finlandese
India/Indian	India/indiano/a
Ireland/Irish	Irlanda/irlandese
Kenya/Kenyan	Kenya/keniota
Nigeria/Nigerian	Nigeria/nigeriano/a
Norway/Norwegian	Norvegia/norvegese
Pakistan/Pakistani	Pakistan/pakistano/a
Philippines/Filipino	Filippine/filippino/a
Scotland/Scottish	Scozia/scozzese
South Africa/South African	Sudafrica/sudafricano/a
Sweden/Swedish	Svezia/svedese
United States/American	Stati Uniti/americano/a
Wales/Welsh	Galles/gallese

D. WORK

For examples of some of the most common jobs/professions → **8. Looking for work**.

I work as a waiter in a bar.	Lavoro come cameriere in un bar.
I'm a chef in a restaurant in Genova.	Faccio il cuoco in un ristorante di Genova.
I'm an office cleaner.	Faccio le pulizie negli uffici.
I do the cleaning for a family.	Faccio la donna di servizio/ l'uomo delle pulizie in una famiglia.
I'm a mechanic in a service area/ petrol station.	Faccio il meccanico in una stazione di servizio.
I work for an automobile company.	Sono operaio in un'azienda automobilistica.

I'm a nurse in a large hospital.	Faccio l'infermiera in un grande ospedale.
I'm a secretary in a legal firm.	Sono segretaria in uno studio di avvocati.
I'm an engineer in an engineering company.	Sono ingegnere in un'azienda metalmeccanica.
I like/don't like my job.	Mi piace/Non mi piace il mio lavoro.
I earn quite a lot/I don't earn enough.	Guadagno abbastanza bene/troppo poco.
I get a good salary, but my job's boring.	Il mio stipendio è buono, ma faccio un lavoro noioso.
My job's interesting but tiring.	Il mio lavoro è interessante, ma faticoso.
I work every day and don't get much time off.	Lavoro tutti i giorni e non ho molto tempo libero.
I work from 9 to 6.	Lavoro dalle 9 del mattino alle 6 del pomeriggio.
I don't work Saturdays.	Sono libera al sabato.

E. RELIGION

I'm/I'm not Catholic.	Sono/Non sono cattolico.
I'm Protestant/Jewish/Muslim/Buddhist/Hindu.	Sono protestante/ebreo/musulmano/buddista/induista.
Is there a Protestant church/synagogue/mosque?	C'è una chiesa protestante/una sinagoga/una moschea?
What time is mass on Sundays?	Qual è l'orario delle messe alla domenica?
What time does the service start?	A che ora è la funzione?
Where is the cathedral?	Dov'è il duomo/la cattedrale?
Is there a priest who speaks English?	C'è un prete che parla inglese?
Is there a Jewish/Muslim community here in the city?	C'è una comunità ebraica/musulmana in questa città?

F. LIKES AND DISLIKES

I like music/sport.	Mi piace la musica/lo sport.
I like going out with my friends.	Mi piace uscire con i miei amici.
I'd like to go to a basketball/football match.	Mi piacerebbe assistere a una partita di pallacanestro/calcio.
I love jazz/rock music.	Adoro il jazz/il rock.
What I really like is rap/football.	Quello che mi appassiona veramente è il rap/il foot-ball.
I love travelling.	Ho sempre voglia di viaggiare.
I like living in the city/the countryside/by the sea.	Mi piace vivere in città/in campagna/al mare.
I miss the weather where I come from.	Del mio paese mi manca tanto il clima.
I'm not interested in politics.	La politica non mi attira.
I prefer jogging/swimming.	Preferisco fare jogging/nuotare.
I hate winter.	Odio l'inverno.
I can't stand fog.	Non sopporto la nebbia.

G. FEELINGS

I'm happy.	Sono contento/a.
I like you/it.	Mi piaci/Mi fa piacere.
You're kind/nice/pretty.	Sei gentile/simpatico/carina.
I get on well with you.	Sto bene con te.
I like you a lot.	Mi piaci molto.
I'm very fond of you.	Ti voglio bene.
I love you.	Ti amo.
I hope you are (being) honest.	Spero che tu sia sincero.
That's nice!	Che bello!
Excellent!/Splendid!	Ottimo!/Splendido!
Well done!	Bravo!/Brava!

I'm unhappy/angry.	**Sono scontento/arrabbiato.**
I'm sorry, I'm afraid that's not possible.	**Mi rincresce, temo che sia impossibile.**
I don't want to.	**Non voglio.**
I don't like him/her/it.	**Non mi piace.**
I don't like doing it.	**Non mi fa piacere.**
I don't like it here. I'm bored.	**Non mi trovo bene qui/ Mi annoio.**
I don't get on with you.	**Non mi trovo bene con te.**
You're not nice.	**Non sei gentile.**
I don't like you.	**Non mi piaci.**
I hate you.	**Ti odio.**
What a shame!	**(Che) Peccato!**
How awful!	**Che orrore!**

6 TRAVELLING

A. ASKING FOR AND GIVING DIRECTIONS

Have you got a map of the city, please?	Ha una piantina della città, per favore?
Where's the centre/… street/… square?	Dov'è il centro/via…/piazza…?
I'm looking for this address.	Cerco questo indirizzo.
Excuse me, which way for the station?	Scusi, che strada devo prendere per andare alla stazione?
Can you tell me how to get to via Roma?	Sa dirmi come arrivare in via Roma?
Keep straight on.	Vada sempre dritto.
Take the first left/right.	Prenda la prima a sinistra/a destra.
Turn right at the second traffic lights.	Giri a destra al secondo semaforo.
Is there a hotel/restaurant near here?	C'è un albergo/un ristorante nei dintorni?

B. PUBLIC TRANSPORT IN THE CITY

Tickets are not sold on buses, trams etc. but can be bought at tobacconists, newsstands and automatic ticket machines. In many large towns you can buy *settimanali* – blocks of 10 tickets – at a slightly reduced rate which are valid on the entire public transport network.

Where's the bus stop/tram stop/coach station?	Dov'è la fermata dell'autobus/del tram/la stazione dei pullman?

How often is there a bus?	Ogni quanto passa l'autobus?
When's the last metro?	A che ora passa l'ultimo metrò?
When does the coach leave?	A che ora parte il pullman?
I'd like a ticket/a book of tickets/ a weekly pass.	Vorrei un biglietto/un blocchetto di biglietti/un settimanale.
Does this tram stop near the police station?	Questo tram si ferma vicino alla questura?
Excuse me, where do I get off for the town hall?	Scusi, dove devo scendere per il municipio?
Where's the terminal?	Dov'è il capolinea?
Where's the nearest metro station?	Dov'è la stazione della metropolitana più vicina?
Which way do I need to go for the hospital?	Che direzione devo prendere per l'ospedale?
Which bus goes to the stadium?	Qual è l'autobus per lo stadio?
Do I need to change? Which stop?	Devo cambiare? A che fermata?
Let me off here, please.	Mi faccia scendere qui, per favore.
Is there a taxi rank nearby?	C'è un posteggio di taxi qui vicino?

C. TRAVELLING BY CAR

Tolls have to be paid on motorways in Italy. At the entrance to the motorway you are given a ticket showing where you joined the motorway. At the exit you pay according to the distance travelled. The speed limit on motorways is 130 kph.
On main roads outside the towns the maximum speed limit – unless otherwise indicated – is 90 kph. In the city it is 50 kph.

Where's the nearest car park?	Dov'è il parcheggio più vicino?
Can you park here? For how long?	Si può parcheggiare qui? Per quanto tempo?
Which road do I take for Cuneo?	Può indicarmi la strada per Cuneo?

Where do I get onto the motorway?	Dov'è l'ingresso dell'autostrada?
Is the service station far?	È lontana la stazione di servizio?
Could you fill it up please?	Mi fa il pieno, per favore?
Can you check the oil and water?	Può controllare acqua e olio?
My car's broken down.	Ho un guasto alla macchina.
My car's run out of petrol.	Sono rimasto senza benzina.
My car won't go.	Non mi parte la macchina.
I've got a puncture/The brakes won't work.	Ho bucato una gomma/I freni non funzionano.
Can you get me a breakdown truck/a mechanic?	Si può avere un carro attrezzi/ un meccanico?
I've had an accident.	Ho avuto un incidente.
It wasn't my fault. She/He didn't give way.	Non è colpa mia. È lei/lui che non ha rispettato la precedenza.
I'm sorry. You're right. I didn't see the (no entry/no parking) sign.	Ha ragione, agente, mi dispiace. Non ho visto il cartello di divieto.
Here are my documents.	Ecco i miei documenti.
Do I have to pay a fine?	Devo pagare una contravvenzione?
I'd like to rent a car.	Vorrei noleggiare una macchina.
How much is it per day? Is insurance included?	Quanto costa al giorno? L'assicurazione è compresa?
What's the charge per kilometre? Is unlimited mileage included?	Qual è la tariffa a km? Il chilometraggio è compreso?

D. BY TRAIN

Always remember to stamp your ticket before getting on the train – there are special machines for this on the platforms. You will be fined if you forget!

Where is the ticket office/ left-luggage office?	Dov'è la biglietteria/ il deposito bagagli?
Are there any luggage lockers?	Ci sono armadietti per depositare i bagagli?

Are there any luggage trolleys?	Ci sono carrelli portabagagli?
What time does the next train for Naples leave?	A che ora parte il prossimo treno per Napoli?
Does the train stop at Spoleto?	Il treno si ferma a Spoleto?
What time does the train from Genova/to Trento arrive?	A che ora arriva il treno da Genova/per Trento?
Do I have to change?	Devo cambiare?
What time is the connection for Piacenza?	A che ora è la coincidenza per Piacenza?
Do I need to book?	La prenotazione è obbligatoria?
I'd like to book two seats.	Vorrei prenotare due posti.
How much is a second-class ticket to Salerno?	Quanto costa un biglietto di seconda classe per Salerno?
I'd like a single ticket/a return ticket in first/second class to Brescia.	Vorrei un biglietto di sola andata/di andata e ritorno in prima/seconda classe per Brescia.
Are there any couchettes left for Palermo?	Ci sono ancora cuccette per Palermo?
Excuse me, is this seat free?	Scusi, è libero questo posto?
I'm sorry, this seat is reserved.	Mi scusi, questo posto è prenotato.
Can I smoke/turn off the light?	Posso fumare/spegnere la luce?
Do you mind closing the window?	Le dispiace chiudere il finestrino?
What time do we arrive in Venice?	A che ora arriviamo a Venezia?
Is the train late?	Siamo in ritardo?
I'm sorry, I forgot to stamp my ticket.	Mi dispiace, ho dimenticato di convalidare il biglietto.

E. BY AIR

I'd like to reserve a seat in economy class on the 20.30 flight for Bari tomorrow.	Vorrei prenotare un posto in classe turistica sull'aereo delle 20.30 di domani per Bari.
Is there a flight to Torino?	C'è un volo per Torino?

What time is the first flight for Roma?	A che ora parte il primo volo per Roma?
The flight's late/been cancelled.	Il volo è in ritardo/annullato.
Where can I check in?	Dov'è il check-in?
How much luggage am I allowed?	Quanti chili di bagaglio si possono portare?
Can I take this bag as hand-luggage?	Posso tenere questa borsa come bagaglio a mano?
Please can you help me? One of my suitcases is missing.	Può aiutarmi, per favore? Mi manca una valigia.
Is there a bus service into the city?	C'è un servizio di autobus per la città?
I've missed my plane. Can I get my ticket refunded or use it again?	Ho perso l'aereo. Posso farmi rimborsare il biglietto o riutilizzarlo?

F. POLICE AND CUSTOMS

Passport, please!	Passaporto, prego.
Here are the car documents.	Ecco i documenti della macchina.
Anything to declare?	Ha qualcosa da dichiarare?
No, nothing to declare.	No, non ho niente da dichiarare.
Yes, a carton of cigarettes and two bottles of wine.	Sì, una stecca di sigarette e due bottiglie di vino.
This suitcase isn't mine.	Questa valigia non è mia.
I'm just passing through. I'm going to Brussels.	Sono di passaggio, vado a Bruxelles.
How much money do you have with you?	Quanto denaro ha con sé?
You have to pay duty.	Deve pagare la dogana.

7 EATING AND DRINKING

In Italy, it is possible to eat reasonably cheaply in the **trattorie** and the **tavole calde** as well as the **ristoranti**. *Pizza* – the best-known Italian speciality – can be found in the numerous **pizzerie**, but sometimes only in the evenings, especially in the south of Italy. In bars and cafés you can get coffee, soft drinks and alcoholic drinks and sandwiches, hot and cold dishes, desserts and ice creams to eat. In the **rosticcerie** you can buy cooked dishes to take away. Nowadays, especially in the large towns, there are an increasing number of restaurants and eating places selling foreign foods such as Asian, African, and Indian.

Lunch is usually between 12.30 and 14.30 whereas dinner is between 19.00 and 21.00 (but often later in the south of Italy).

Setting the table

ashtray	il portacenere
cup	la tazza
cutlery	le posate
fork	la forchetta
glass	il bicchiere
knife	il coltello
napkin	la tovaglia
plate/dish	il piatto
spoon	il cucchiaio
tablecloth	il tovagliolo
teaspoon	il cucchiaino

Meals and courses

breakfast	la prima colazione
lunch	il pranzo

dinner	la cena
starter	l'antipasto
first/second course	il primo/il secondo piatto
meat	la carne
fish	il pesce
vegetables/side dish	il contorno
dessert	il dolce
fruit	la frutta

Food

bread	il pane
broth/soup	la minestra in brodo/la zuppa
cheese	il formaggio
milk	il latte
pasta/spaghetti	la pasta/gli spaghetti
rice	il riso
veal/beef/lamb/pork/chicken/turkey	la carne di vitello/manzo/agnello/maiale/pollo/tacchino

Taste and food quality

bitter	amaro
hot/spicy	piccante
insipid/tasteless	insipido
salty	salato
sour	acido/aspro
sweet	dolce
tasty	saporito
fat(ty)	grasso
heavy	pesante
lean	magro
light	leggero

Methods of cooking

barbequed	allo spiedo
boiled	bollito/lesso
cold/hot	freddo/caldo
fried	fritto
grilled	ai ferri/alla griglia
rare/well-done	al sangue/ben cotto
raw/cooked	crudo/cotto
steamed	al vapore
with a sauce	con la salsa

Condiments and spices

butter	il burro
cream	la panna
garlic	l'aglio
margarine	la margarina
mayonnaise	la maionese
mustard	la senape
olive oil/vegetable oil	l'olio d'oliva/l'olio di semi
pepper	il pepe
salt	il sale
sugar	lo zucchero
vinegar	l'aceto
cinnamon	la cannella
cloves	i chiodi di garofano
hot red pepper	il peperoncino
nutmeg	la noce moscata
paprika	la paprika
saffron	lo zafferano

A. IN THE BAR

(A) coffee, please.	Un caffè espresso, per favore.
I'd like a cappucino and a brioche.	Vorrei un cappuccino e una brioche.

A draught beer and a fruit juice, please.	Una birra alla spina e un succo di frutta. Grazie.
Could I have a ham sandwich and a coke, please?	Per favore, mi porti un panino al prosciutto e una coca-cola.
We will have a chocolate and a strawberry and lemon ice-cream.	Vorremmo un gelato al cioccolato e uno fragola e limone.
(We had) A glass of white wine and two teas. How much is that?	Abbiamo preso un bicchiere di vino bianco e due tè. Quanto è/ Quanto pago?
It's my turn.	Offro io questo giro.
Cheers!	Alla salute!

B. AT LUNCH/DINNER

Where am I sitting?	Qual è il mio posto?
Where shall I sit?	Dove posso sedermi?
Sit between us.	Siediti tra noi due.
Sit down beside me.	Si sieda vicino a me.
Can you pass me the salt?	Mi passi il sale?
Is there any pepper, please?	C'è il pepe, per favore?
Could I have some bread?	Posso avere del pane?
Can I serve you?	Posso servirla?

C. AT THE RESTAURANT

I'd like to book a table for two for tomorrow evening at 8.	Vorrei prenotare un tavolo per due persone per domani sera alle 8.
Is there a table free/in the garden/on the terrace?	C'è un tavolo libero/in giardino/ sulla terrazza?
Could we have a menu, please?	Ci porta il menù, per favore?
Have you got a tourist menu?	Avete un menù turistico?
Have you got a regional/house speciality?	Avete specialità della regione/ della casa?

What do you recommend?	Può darmi un consiglio?
What is this (dish)?	Può spiegarmi questo piatto?
What's the special of the day?	Qual è il piatto del giorno?
I'd like a grilled steak with chips/courgettes/peas/salad/tomatoes.	Vorrei una bistecca alla griglia con patate fritte/zucchini/piselli/insalata/pomodori.
I'd like a carafe of white/red wine and a bottle of mineral water.	Vorrei una caraffa di vino bianco/rosso e una bottiglia di acqua minerale.
Is service included?	Il servizio è compreso?
Could you bring me the bill, please?/The bill, please.	Mi porta il conto, per favore?/Il conto, per favore.
Excuse me, there's a mistake in the bill. I didn't have any wine.	Mi scusi, ma c'è un errore nel conto. Non ho preso vino.

D. TASTES AND PREFERENCES

Do you like it?/Don't you like it?	Ti piace?/Non ti piace?
I like it.	Mi piace.
It's very good!	È molto buono!/Che buono!
Do you like the vegetables done like that?	Le piacciono le verdure cucinate così?
Sorry, it's too salty/spicy for me.	Mi scusi, ma è troppo salato/piccante per me.
Would you like some more?	Ne vuoi ancora un po'?
Can I help you to some more meat?	Posso servirle ancora un po' di carne?
Thank you, I'll have a little more.	Grazie, ne prendo ancora un po'.
No, thank you, I've had enough.	No grazie, ho mangiato abbastanza/già troppo.
I'd prefer the pasta, thanks.	Preferisco la pasta, grazie.
My favourite food is pizza.	Il mio piatto preferito è la pizza.
I like eating well.	Sono un buongustaio/Mi piace mangiare bene.

I eat a lot.	Sono una buona forchetta/ Mangio molto.
I'm vegetarian.	Sono vegetariano.
I'm not used to such hot/spicy food.	Non sono abituato ai sapori così forti.
I can't eat salame.	Non posso mangiare il salame.
I'm afraid I don't eat meat.	Mi dispiace, non mangio carne.
Unfortunately I don't like fish.	Purtroppo non mi piace il pesce.
Would you like some wine?	Gradisce del vino?
Yes, please!/No, thanks, I don't drink wine.	Sì, grazie!/No, grazie, non bevo vino.
What will you have for dessert?	Che cosa prende come dessert?

8 LOOKING FOR WORK

The situations vacant columns in the local and daily newspapers are good places to look for work. You can also put in your own (paid) job ad. (→ **18**. **Classified advertisements**: A. Jobs). You can write directly to the large companies and managers of shops and restaurants and send them your CV. (→ **17. Writing**: E. Curriculum vitae/ CV). Word of mouth of friends and acquaintances is also useful.

Jobs and professions

accountant	contabile
apprentice	apprendista
bricklayer	muratore
chef	cuoco/a
cleaner/cleaning lady	uomo/donna delle pulizie
dishwasher	lavapiatti
driver	autista
dustman	spazzino
mechanic	meccanico
office worker	impiegato/a
painter and decorator	imbianchino
postman	postino/a
secretary	segretaria
shop assistant	commesso/a
(switchboard) operator	centralinista
waiter/waitress	cameriere/a
worker	operaio/a

A. GETTING THE INFORMATION YOU NEED

I'm looking for work.	Sto cercando lavoro.

I need work. Do you have anything in your company?	Ho bisogno di lavorare. C'è qualche possibilità in questa azienda?
Do you need anyone?	Manca personale?
Do you need waiters/workers/office staff?	Avete bisogno di camerieri/operai/impiegati?
Do you know if they need anyone here?	Mi sa dire se qui c'è richiesta di manodopera?
Who do I need to see about working here?	A chi devo rivolgermi per un eventuale impiego?
Where should I ask?	Dove devo presentarmi?
I'd like to apply for the job.	Vorrei fare domanda d'assunzione.
I saw your vacancy for a deliveryman (in the newspaper).	Ho letto il vostro annuncio per un posto di fattorino.

B. GIVING INFORMATION ABOUT YOURSELF

I don't speak Italian well, but I'm studying it.	Non parlo bene l'italiano, ma lo sto studiando.
I speak Italian (quite) well.	Parlo (abbastanza) bene l'italiano.
I left school at 14.	Ho studiato fino a 14 anni.
I've got a diploma in accountancy/secretarial training.	Ho un diploma di ragioniere/una preparazione da segretaria.
I was a dishwasher and waiter in a restaurant in Roma.	Ho fatto il lavapiatti e il cameriere in un ristorante di Roma.
I already work as a house maid three days a week.	Lavoro già come domestica/donna delle pulizie tre giorni alla settimana.
Before coming here I worked as a gardener.	Al mio paese lavoravo come giardiniere.
I worked for six months in the automobile industry.	Ho lavorato sei mesi come operaio nel settore automobilistico.
I worked for three years in accounting/in production.	Ho un'esperienza di tre anni in contabilità/in produzione.

At the moment I'm working as a clerk/in charge of warehouse and handling in a packing company.	Attualmente ho un posto di impiegato/sono addetto al magazzino e alla movimentazione in una ditta di imballaggi.
I'd like to be a seller/work in a… company.	Mi piacerebbe fare il venditore/lavorare in una ditta di…
I'm willing to do shifts/any hours.	Sono disponibile per qualsiasi turno/qualsiasi orario.
I'm available in the mornings/afternoons/all day.	Sono libero la mattina/il pomeriggio/tutto il giorno.
I learn quickly.	Imparo in fretta.
I want to work.	Ho voglia di lavorare.
I have references.	Posso dare delle referenze.

C. ASKING FOR DETAILS ABOUT WORK

What would I have to do?	Che cosa dovrei fare?
Could you tell me exactly what I would have to do?	Può dirmi quali sarebbero esattamente i miei compiti?
Where's the job?/What are the hours of work?	Qual è la sede/l'orario di lavoro?
When do I begin?	Quando incomincio?
Who will I be working with?	Con chi dovrei lavorare?
Who is my immediate boss?	Chi è il mio superiore diretto?
What do I have to do?	Quali sono le mie responsabilità?
How long will this job probably last?	Quanto durerebbe all'incirca questo incarico?
Will there be overtime?	Sono previsti straordinari?
When is my day off?	Qual è il giorno libero?
Will it be possible to take time off for university?	Sarebbe possibile prendere permessi per l'università?
How many days off am I entitled to? Starting when?	A quanti giorni di ferie ho diritto? A partire da quando?
Will I be able to improve my starting position?	Ci sono possibilità di migliorare la posizione di partenza?

D. ASKING FOR CLARIFICATION ON PAY

Will I be taken on regularly or 'on the black'?	Sarei assunto regolarmente o lavorerei in nero?
Might I be taken on regularly later?	C'è la possibilità di essere assunto regolarmente più tardi?
What's the hourly/daily pay?	Qual è la paga oraria/giornaliera?
What's the net/gross pay per week/month.	Qual è la retribuzione netta/lorda alla settimana/al mese?
O.K. I accept/No thanks. I don't want it.	Va bene, accetto/No, grazie. Non accetto.
When are the salaries paid?	Quando viene pagato lo stipendio?
How are the salaries paid? In cash?	In che modo viene versato lo stipendio? In contanti?
It doesn't seem much (pay) for such hard work.	La paga mi sembra bassa per un lavoro così faticoso.
I want to earn more.	Vorrei guadagnare di più.
Could I expect a pay rise before long?	Posso sperare in un aumento di stipendio a breve termine?
They're long hours so I think the salary should be higher.	Credo che il compenso dovrebbe essere più elevato, visto l'orario di lavoro.

9 LOOKING FOR ACCOMODATION

You can find furnished rooms or flats to rent or buy by reading the house advertisements in the daily newspapers and specialised journals. Or go to a house agent's. (→ **18. Classified advertisements**: B. Property).
You will often see coloured notices on the main entrance doors to buildings: *Vendesi* (For sale) and *Affittasi* (To let/rent).

balcony	il balcone
bathroom	il bagno
bedroom	la camera da letto
bedsit/one-roomed flat	il monolocale
caretaker	il portinaio, la portinaia
caretaker's lodge	la portineria
contract	il contratto
courtyard	il cortile
deposit	l'anticipo/la caparra
dining room	la sala da pranzo
flat	l'appartamento
floor (ist/2nd/3rd etc.)	il piano
furnished/non-furnished	arredato/non arredato
furnishings/furniture	l'arredamento
garage	il box
heating	il riscaldamento
home	l'abitazione
house	la casa
kitchen	la cucina
lift	l'ascensore
(to) move	cambiare casa
radiator	il calorifero

(to) rent	affittare
rent	l'affitto
room	il locale/la stanza
sitting room	il soggiorno
tenant	l'inquilino

Furniture

armchair	la poltrona
chairs	le sedie
cupboards	i mobiletti/i pensili
fridge	il frigorifero
furniture	l'arredamento
gas cooker	la cucina a gas
sofa	il divano
single/double bed	il letto singolo/matrimoniale
table	il tavolo
wardrobe	l'armadio

A. EXPLAINING WHAT YOU WANT

I'm looking for a flat.	Sto cercando casa.
Do you have a room to rent?	Avete una camera da affittare?
I'm from India and I want to stay in Genova for six months.	Vengo dall'India e vorrei rimanere a Genova sei mesi.
I'd like cheap accomodation, even if it's in an old house.	Vorrei una sistemazione economica, anche in una casa vecchia.
I'm looking for a furnished room with use of kitchen to rent.	Cerco in affitto una camera ammobiliata con uso cucina.
I'd like a bigger/smaller/lighter/quieter/more comfortable room, which looks onto the courtyard/street.	Vorrei una camera più grande/piccola/luminosa/tranquilla/comoda, che dia sul cortile/su strada.
Do you have an inexpensive furnished/non furnished bedsit near the centre?	Può propormi un monolocale arredato/non arredato, non troppo caro, vicino al centro?

There are four of us so we'd like a two-roomed flat with bathroom and a terrace or garden.	Siamo in quattro, e vorremmo un appartamento di due locali più servizi, con un terrazzo o un giardino.
I'd prefer the area near the station to be closer to work.	Preferirei la zona della stazione, per non essere troppo lontano dal mio lavoro.

B. GETTING THE INFORMATION YOU NEED

Which area is it in? Is it close/far from the centre?	In che zona si trova? È vicino/lontano dal centro?
What floor is it on?	A che piano è?
Is there a lift/caretaker's lodge?	C'è l'ascensore/la portineria?
Is it centralised or autonomous heating?	Il riscaldamento è centralizzato o autonomo?
Will I be able to cook?	C'è la possibilità di cucinare?
Is the room furnished? How?	La camera è ammobiliata? Come?
How is the flat laid out?	Come è composto l'appartamento?
How many rooms are there?/How many bedrooms?	Quanti locali ci sono?/Quante camere da letto?
Is there a cellar or an attic?	C'è una cantina o un solaio?
Can I see the room/flat?	Posso vedere la camera/l'appartamento?
Is it well-served by public transport?	È servito bene dai mezzi pubblici?
Is there a tram/bus/metro stop nearby?	Ci sono fermate dei tram/degli autobus/della metropolitana vicine?
When can I move into the flat?	Quando potrò occupare l'appartamento?

C. DISCUSSING THE FORMALITIES

How much is the rent?	Quant'è l'affitto?
Are all charges/Is the heating included in the price?	Le spese/il riscaldamento sono compresi nel prezzo?

Is the rent to be paid in advance?	L'affitto si paga anticipato?
Is a deposit required?	Bisogna versare una caparra?
How long is the contract for? Is it renewable?	Che durata ha il contratto? È rinnovabile?
When can we sign the contract?	Quando possiamo firmare il contratto?
How much is it to buy?	Qual è il prezzo d'acquisto?
How do I have to pay?	Come deve essere effettuato il pagamento?

10 DOMESTIC PROBLEMS

A. UTILITIES

When you move into a flat you have to contact the companies which furnish the telephone (*servizio telefonico*), water supply (*erogazione di acqua*), electricity (*energia elettrica*) and gas (*gas*). You need to contact these same companies in case of installation or other problems and to close the contract and (water/electricity/gas) supply when you leave the flat.

I'm about to move into a flat and I want to know what I need to do to have the electricity/gas/water connected?	Sto per entrare in un appartamento e vorrei sapere che cosa devo fare per avere l'allacciamento all'impianto elettrico/del gas/dell'acqua potabile.
I'm about to move house. Can you tell me what I have to do to get a phone?	Sto per cambiare casa; può dirmi quali sono le formalità per avere il telefono?
It's a new contract/I'm taking over somebody's contract.	Si tratta di un nuovo contratto/di un subentro nella fornitura.
Which office do I need to go to?	A che ufficio devo rivolgermi?
Can you give me the phone number?	Può darmi il numero di telefono?
What are the (office) opening hours?	Quali sono gli orari (degli sportelli)?
What documents do I need?	Quali documenti sono necessari?
Is there long to wait?	C'è molto da aspettare?
How much will it be? Do I need to pay in advance?	Quanto viene a costare? Bisogna pagare in anticipo?

How much is the fixed rent?	Quant'è il canone fisso?
Could I make an appointment?	È possibile fissare un appuntamento?
I'd like to close my contract. The contract number is… and it is in my name.	Vorrei dare la disdetta della fornitura. Il contratto ha il numero… ed è intestato a me.
I'll give you the last meter reading.	Le do l'ultima lettura del contatore.
My phone isn't working.	Il mio telefono non funziona.
I need to report a broken… Can you see to it or do you need to send someone out?	Devo segnalare un guasto. Potete risolverlo dalla centrale o dovete mandare qualcuno?
I can smell gas in the building/ flat.	C'è odore di gas nel palazzo/ nell'appartamento.
I've got a gas/water leak.	C'è una perdita di gas/acqua.
We're without electricity.	Siamo rimasti senza corrente elettrica.

B. PROBLEMS AND REPAIRS

For problems with sanitary ware (*apparecchi idrosanitari*) and household appliances (*elettrodomestici*) you need to contact a plumber (*idraulico*) or an electrician (*elettricista*).

The sink/bidet/toilet is blocked/ leaking.	Il lavandino/il bidé/il water è otturato/perde.
The washing machine/ dishwasher isn't working/has stopped working.	La lavatrice/la lavastoviglie non funziona più/si è fermata.
The house is flooded.	La casa si è allagata.
The fridge won't cool down.	Il frigorifero non raffredda.
Can you come to look at/repair the boiler? When?	Può venire a vedere/riparare lo scaldabagno? Quando?
Tell me what time you can come then someone can be in.	Può dirmi verso che ora, dato che lavoriamo tutti?

They said they would send someone on Wednesday. Today's Friday but nobody's come yet.	Aveva detto che avrebbe mandato il tecnico mercoledì, ma è venerdì e non è ancora venuto nessuno.
Please! It's urgent!	Per favore, è urgente!
How much is the spare part? Can you give me an estimate for the job?	Quanto costa il pezzo di ricambio? Può farmi un preventivo del lavoro?
How long will it take to repair it? Is it worth mending?	Quanto tempo ci vuole per fare la riparazione? Vale la pena di aggiustarlo?

C. GETTING ON WITH YOUR NEIGHBOURS

• When you rent or buy a flat in a block of flats, you are advised to maintain good and, if possible, friendly relations (*rapporti cortesi*) with the other flat owners (*condomini*).

Excuse me, the wind/storm blew my washing/brush onto your balcony. Can I come and get it?	Mi scusi, ma il vento/il temporale ha fatto cadere il bucato/la scopa sul suo balcone. Posso riprenderli?
I'm sorry for all the noise/coming and going this afternoon. It's the baby's christening/birthday and we've invited a few friends.	La prego di scusarmi per il chiasso/il viavai di questo pomeriggio. È il battesimo/compleanno del bambino e abbiamo invitato alcuni amici.
I'm really sorry about the damp patches in your flat; the washing machine tube broke. I've already told the insurance company and they'll contact you as soon as possible.	Mi dispiace molto per le macchie di umidità nel suo appartamento. Si è rotto il tubo della lavatrice. Ho già informato l'assicurazione che la contatterà al più presto.
Please could you turn the TV/stereo down? Unfortunately the walls are very thin and I have to get up early in the morning.	Per favore, può abbassare il volume del suo televisore/stereo? Purtroppo le pareti sono molto sottili e alla mattina mi alzo sempre prestissimo.
When you water the flowers, the water drips onto my balcony. Could you be more careful?	Quando innaffia i fiori, bagna sempre il mio balcone. La prego di fare più attenzione.

I can assure you that we're not responsible for the noise you hear during the night. Perhaps it's the people above. Try asking them.

Le assicuro che non siamo noi i responsabili del rumore che la disturba di notte. Forse saranno gli inquilini del piano di sopra. Provi a chiedere a loro.

• Requests and complaints to the landlord (*padrone di casa*) should also be made politely.

I want to tell you that the heating isn't working properly. The house is cold.

Vorrei segnalarle che il riscaldamento non funziona bene. In casa fa freddo.

Excuse me, the front door/ bedroom window doesn't close properly. Could you send someone to repair it?

Mi scusi, la porta d'ingresso/la finestra della camera non chiude bene. Potrebbe mandare qualcuno a ripararla?

I'm afraid the sitting room windowpane is broken. What should I do?

Sono desolata, ma si è rotto un vetro della finestra della sala. Che cosa devo fare?

I've got one or two problems at the moment. Could I ask you to postpone payment of the rent for a week?

In questo momento ho qualche problema. Posso chiederle di rimandare di una settimana il pagamento dell'affitto?

11 SHOPPING AND SERVICES

bargain	un'occasione
buy	acquistare/comprare
credit card	la carta di credito
department	il reparto
discount	lo sconto
escalator	la scala mobile
floor (1st/2nd etc.)	il piano
price	il prezzo
purchase/shopping	l'acquisto
rent/hire	affittare/noleggiare
sales	i saldi
second-hand	usato/di seconda mano
sell	vendere
shop	il negozio
shop assistant	il commesso/la commessa
spend	spendere
till/checkout	la cassa

Shops

baker's	la panetteria
butcher's	la macelleria
cake shop	la pasticceria
chemist's	la farmacia
dairy	la latteria
delicatessen	la salumeria
greengrocer's	il fruttivendolo/l'ortolano
grocer's	la drogheria

hairdresser's	il parrucchiere
hardware store	il negozio di ferramenta
launderette/dry cleaner's	la lavanderia/la tintoria
market	il mercato
newsstand	l'edicola
perfumery	la profumeria
stationer's	la cartoleria
tobacconist's	la tabaccheria

A. SHOPPING FOR FOOD AND HOUSEHOLD GOODS

In large towns the food shops (*negozi*) are constantly being re-
placed by supermarkets (*supermercati*), where you can buy food
and household goods at fairly reasonable prices. Even bigger and
better stocked are the hypermarkets (*ipermercati*), which are generally to be found in the outlying districts of the city. Even in the
smaller centres, a growing number of mini supermarkets now sell
a vast assortment of products, so the traditional distinction between one shop and another is being lost.
All loose products are sold in *chilogrammi* (for solids) and in *litri* (for
liquids).

At the shops

Is there any bread left?	C'è ancora pane?
I'll have some French bread and a kilo of pasta, please.	Mi dia un filone di pane e un chilo di pasta, per favore.
I'd like some sugar, a jar of strawberry jam and a tin of biscuits.	Vorrei un pacco di zucchero, un vasetto di marmellata di fragole e una scatola di biscotti.
A kilo of potatoes, a kilo of oranges and a lettuce, please.	Per favore, un chilo di patate, un chilo di arance e un cespo di lattuga.
Have you got any fresh peas and apricots?	Ha dei piselli freschi e delle albicocche?
How much is a kilo of grapes?	Quanto costa l'uva al chilo?

I'd like a kilo/half a kilo of lamb and 300 grams of mince.	Vorrei un chilo/mezzo chilo di carne di agnello e tre etti di carne trita di manzo.
A litre of milk, please. And 200 grams of cooked/parma ham.	Mi dà un litro di latte, per favore? E anche due etti di prosciutto cotto/crudo.
How much is that/do I owe you?	Quanto pago?/le devo?
I'm waiting for the change.	Sto aspettando il resto.
Can I have a plastic bag?	Può darmi un sacchetto di plastica?

At the supermarket

Can you give me some change for the trolley?	Può cambiarmi delle monete per il carrello?
Is there a frozen food section?	C'è il reparto surgelati?
Where is the delicatessen counter?	Dov'è il reparto salumeria?
Where can I find the toilet paper, please?	Dove posso trovare la carta igienica, per favore?
I need this detergent. Do you have it?	Mi serve questo detersivo. L'avete?
I'm looking for this brand of coffee. Do you stock it?	Sto cercando questa marca di caffè? La vendete?

B. DEPARTMENT STORES

In all major towns the department stores (*grandi magazzini*) offer a large selection of products ranging from clothes to perfumes to jewellery and household goods. In the various departments (*reparti*), easily visible signs indicate the articles for sale on that floor.

Can I look around?	Posso dare un'occhiata?
Can you help me?	Può aiutarmi?
Can I see the jumper in the window?	Può mostrarmi il golf che è in vetrina?

Excuse me, which floor is the lingerie department on?	Per favore, a che piano è il reparto biancheria?
Good morning! I'd like to buy a pair of jeans.	Buongiorno! Vorrei comprare un paio di jeans.
Can I try them on? I take size 44.	Posso provarli? Porto la 44.
I'd like to see some men's cotton shirts, please.	Vorrei vedere delle camicie da uomo in cotone, per favore.
Can I see something else?	Può mostrarmi qualcos'altro?
These trousers don't fit well. They're too big/tight.	Questi pantaloni non mi vanno bene. Sono troppo larghi/stretti.
Do you have a bigger/smaller size?	Ha una taglia più grande/piccola?
What a nice skirt! Have you any other colours?	Che bella gonna! Ha degli altri colori?
I'm looking for a pair of canvas tennis shoes. Blue. I take a 37.	Cerco un paio di scarpe da ginnastica in tela blu. Ho il 37.
Can you tell how much this is?	Mi può dire il prezzo di questo articolo?
O.K. I'll take it.	Va bene, lo prendo.
Have you got anything cheaper?	Ha qualcosa di più economico?
Is there anything in the sale/ on special offer?	C'è qualcosa in saldo/in offerta speciale?
Thanks, but I'll leave it.	Grazie, ma non va bene.

C. SUNDRY

Stamps (*francobolli*) and cigarettes (*sigarette*) are sold both in tobacconist's shops and in bars. The sign to look out for is a large white (sometimes coloured) *T* on a black, white or coloured background.
Newspapers (*giornali*) and magazines are now sold in various outlets. You can buy them at newsstands and newsagents, some bookshops and stationers and in most supermarkets.

Excuse me, where can I buy some stamps/cigarettes?	Scusa, sai dove posso comprare dei francobolli/le sigarette?

A pack/carton of cigarettes and a box of matches, please.	Un pacchetto/una stecca di sigarette e una scatola di fiammiferi, per favore.
Two postcards and two 800 lire stamps, please.	Due cartoline e due francobolli da 800 lire, grazie.
I need to buy a present. Can you advise me?	Devo fare un regalino. Può consigliarmi?
Too much! Have you something less expensive?	Costa troppo. Ha qualcosa di meno caro?
I'll take this bunch of yellow roses.	Prendo questo mazzo di rose gialle.
Do you sell English newspapers?	Avete quotidiani inglesi?
I want this jacket dry-cleaned.	Vorrei far lavare a secco questa giacca.
Could I have these two shirts washed and ironed for tomorrow?	Può lavare e stirare queste due camicie per domani?
Is there a coin-operated launderette?	C'è una lavanderia a gettone?
I need a 50 cc moped to use around the city. Have you got anything cheap?	Mi servirebbe un motorino da 50 cc da usare in città. Ha qualche occasione?
I want to buy a second-hand car/bicycle. Have you got anything?	Vorrei comprare una macchina/una bicicletta di seconda mano. Ha qualcosa da propormi?

D. PAYMENT

Can I pay by credit card/cheque?	Posso pagare con la carta di credito/con un assegno?
What conditions of payment do you offer?	Ci sono condizioni particolari di pagamento?
Is it reduced?	C'è uno sconto?
Do I have to pay the entire amount at the moment of purchase?	È necessario pagare l'importo totale al momento dell'acquisto?

Can I pay by instalments?

È possibile pagare a rate?

How much do I have to pay per month?

Quanto dovrei pagare al mese?

How much does the interest come to?

A quanto ammontano gli interessi?

How much do you want in advance?

Quanto vuole di anticipo?

12 OFFICES AND BUREAUCRACY

A. BUREAUCRATIC LANGUAGE

• Encounters with public administration (*pubblica amministrazione*) and with offices (*uffici*) often create problems because the language is technical and bureaucratic. A lot of vocabulary and expressions which you normally don't hear are used. You need to know these.

l'atto notarile	deed (issued by a notary)
l'autentica	authentication
autenticare	authenticate (a document)
il certificato	certificate
in carta libera	on unstamped paper
in carta da bollo	on stamped paper
compilare	to fill in (a document)
il comune	municipality
il comune di residenza	place of residence
consegnare	deliver/hand in
il consolato	consulate
la denuncia	statement/report (official)
denunciare	report (a crime, a loss, a birth etc.)
in doppia copia	in duplicate
la delega	authorisation(to act as a proxy)
la domanda	application/request/claim
la firma	signature
firmare	sign
iscrivere	register/enter/enrol
l'iscrizione	registration/entry/enrolment
la marca da bollo	revenue stamp

il modulo	form
il notaio	notary
la pratica	paper/case/dossier
presentare	show/produce/present (e.g. birth certificate)
la questura	police headquarters
la ricevuta	receipt
richiedere	apply for/request
la richiesta	application/request
la scadenza	expiry date/deadline
scadere	expire/run out/lapse
sollecitare	request urgently
il sollecito	reminder
il sottoscritto	the undersigned
lo sportello	counter/desk
la tariffa	rate/tariff/charge/fee
la tassa	tax
l'ufficio anagrafe	registry office
l'utente	user/consumer
il versamento	payment
versare	pay in (out)

• It's important to know the names of the documents (*documenti*) and certificates (*certificati*) required in Italy from foreigners.

carta d'identità	identity card
certificato di cittadinanza	certificate of citizenship
certificato di nascita	birth certificate
certificato di residenza	certificate of domicile
certificato di vaccinazione	vaccination certificate
fedina penale	criminal record
libretto di lavoro	employment document
patente	driving licence
permesso di soggiorno	residence permit
servizio militare	military service
stato di famiglia	family status
titolo di studio	educational qualifications

B. INFORMATION

I'd like some information.	Può darmi qualche informazione?
Which office/counter do I need to go to?	A che ufficio/sportello devo rivolgermi per...?
Can I do it by phone?	Si può fare per telefono?
Can you write the address for me?	Può scrivermi l'indirizzo?
When is it open to the public?	Quali sono gli orari d'apertura al pubblico?
Which documents do I need to bring?	Che documenti devo presentare?
Do I have to fill in a form? Can you give me three copies, please?	Devo compilare un modulo? Può darmene tre copie, per favore?
Can you help me to fill in this form, please?	Può aiutami a compilare questo modulo, per favore?
Can I authorise someone to...?	Posso mandare qualcuno con una delega?
How long will it take?	Quanto tempo ci vorrà?
Is it free or do I have to pay something?	È gratuito o bisogna pagare qualcosa?
Can I certify that myself? (i.e. write out a declaration and sign it in the presence of an official)	È valida l'autocertificazione?

C. AT THE POST OFFICE

• Italian post offices (*uffici postali*) can be recognised by the yellow sign **PT** (*Poste e Telegrafo*) or by the new sign *Agenzia postale*. They are open from 8.30 a.m. to 2 p.m., Monday to Friday, and generally until midday on Saturdays. Stamps are also sold at tobacconist's → **11. Shopping and services:** C. Sundry. In the city, the central post office and those situated near the railway stations usually remain open during the afternoon. Letter boxes are red.

I need to send this letter abroad, to Toronto, but I think it weighs too much. What stamps do I	Devo inviare questa lettera all'estero, a Toronto, ma credo che superi il peso. Che

need to put on?	francobolli devo mettere?
Do you know what the postcode for Toronto is?	Sa qual è il codice postale di Toronto?
Can you give me a form to open a post-office account, please?	Può darmi un modulo di conto corrente, per favore?
What do I have to do to send a registered letter with a return receipt?	Che cosa devo fare per spedire una raccomandata con avviso di ricevimento?
How much is it to send this package to London by air mail/express delivery/registered mail?	Quanto costa spedire questo pacco a Londra per via aerea/per espresso/per raccomandata?
How long will it take to get there?	Quanto tempo impiegherà per arrivare?
Excuse me, which is the poste restante counter? I'd like to know if I've got any mail.	Scusi, qual è lo sportello del fermo posta? Vorrei sapere se c'è posta per me.
I have to send a telegram. How much per word is it?	Devo fare un telegramma. Quanto costa a parola?
I want to cash/send an international money-order.	Vorrei incassare/spedire un vaglia internazionale.

• For greater clarity, the most commonly requested operations/forms are given below along with a translation of the terms necessary to fill them out.

CONTO CORRENTE POSTALE (Post-office account)

Intestato a	Made out to...
Eseguito da	Effected by...
Residente in	Domiciled in...
In cifre/in lettere	In figures/in words
Causale del versamento	Description of payment
Compilare in tutte le sue parti, anche sul retro	Each section to be filled in, including overleaf
Non sono ammessi bollettini recanti cancellature, abrasioni o correzioni	Bills and forms with crossings out, erasures and corrections are not accepted

CONTI CORRENTI POSTALI
ATTESTAZIONE di un versamento **di L.** ....

Lire ....

....

sul C/C N. ....

intestato a ....

....

....

eseguito da ....

residente in ....

addì ....

Bollo lineare dell'Ufficio accettante

L'UFFICIALE POSTALE

Bollo a data .... **N.** ....
del bollettario **ch 9**

data   progress.

Mod. 22 - R   cod. 008150

**Poste
Italiane**
Ente Pubblico Economico   **RICEVUTA**

Accettazione RACCOMANDATA

È vietato includere denaro e valori nelle raccomandate: l'Ente Poste non ne risponde

Compilare, a cura del mittente, a macchina o in carattere stampatello

DESTINATARIO DESTINATARIO		
VIA / PIAZZA		N. CIV.
C.A.P.	COMUNE	PROV.
MITTENTE MITTENTE		
VIA / PIAZZA		N. CIV.
C.A.P.	COMUNE	PROV.

| SERVIZI ACCESSORI RICHIESTI Contrassegnare la casella interessata | ☐ Espresso ☐ Assegno L. .... (in cifre) | ☐ Via aerea | ☐ A.R. |

Istituto Poligrafico e Zecca dello Stato - S.N. Roma

RACCOMANDATA A.R. – CON AVVISO DI RICEVIMENTO
(Registered letter with a return receipt)

Destinatario	Addressee
Mittente	Sender
Compilare a macchina o in carattere stampatello	Type or use capital letters
Da restituire a	To return to
Da compilare a cura del mittente	To be filled in by sender
Indirizzata a	Addressed to
Dichiaro di aver ricevuto quanto suindicato	I declare that I have received the above-mentioned (sum/amount etc.)

• The relevant forms to transfer money abroad (*Richiesta di trasferimento di fondi verso l'estero*) can be found at the post office. These forms differ according to the country of destination and they are often filled in at the counter by the clerk on duty. The most important terms to understand are:

Pagamento	Payment
In contanti	In cash
Con accreditamento	To credit your account
Importo da trasferire	Amount to be transferred
Richiedente	Applicant
Beneficiario	Beneficiary
Causale valutaria	Foreign currency payment/ withdrawal
Cognome e nome	Surname and name
Indirizzo	Address
Data di nascita	Date of birth

D. AT THE BANK

The banks are open from 8.30 to 13.30, Monday to Friday, and usually for at least an hour in the afternoon between 14.45 and 16.15 (afternoon hours vary). Exchange offices (*uffici di cambio*) which are open for longer can be found in the railway stations, airports and ports.

I'd like to change this money into lire. What's today's exchange rate?

Vorrei cambiare questi soldi in lire italiane. Qual è il cambio del giorno?

I'd like to cash these traveller's cheques. What commission do you charge?

Vorrei incassare questi traveller's cheque. Quant'è la vostra commissione?

Could I open an account with you?

Posso aprire un conto corrente presso la vostra banca?

My account is with you. I'd like to have a credit card/cashpoint card.

Ho un conto presso di voi. Vorrei avere una carta di credito/una tessera Bancomat.

I'd like to withdraw this amount from/pay this amount into my current account.

Per favore, vorrei prelevare/ versare sul mio conto corrente questa cifra.

I'd like to take out some money. Here's my cashpoint card.

Vorrei ritirare dei soldi. Ecco la mia carta Bancomat.

Which form do I need to make out a transfer?

Che modulo devo compilare per fare un bonifico?

Can I have my electricity and gas bills paid by direct debit?

È possibile domiciliare le bollette di luce e gas presso di voi?

Excuse me, where is there a cashpoint machine?

Scusi, dove posso trovare uno sportello automatico Bancomat?

E. AT THE POLICE HEADQUARTERS/STATION

• Citizens from outside the EEC, as well as citizens from within the EEC who remain in Italy for over three months, have to apply for a work permit (*permesso di soggiorno*) at the police headquarters (*questura*). The relevant office is l'*Ufficio stranieri*, where you also need to go to get the papers to apply for family members to join you in Italy (*ricongiungimento dei familiari*).

I want to apply for a residence permit. I'm from…

Vorrei richiedere il permesso di soggiorno. Sono cittadino…

I need to renew my residence permit.

Devo rinnovare il permesso di soggiorno.

Here's my passport/marriage licence/consular declaration.

Ecco il mio passaporto/certificato di matrimonio/la dichiarazione consolare.

I want to apply for my wife/ (dependent/adult) children to join me.	Vorrei chiedere il ricongiungimento con mia moglie/ i miei figli minorenni/ maggiorenni.
I applied for a residence permit on the 27th March. I have the receipt here. Is it ready?	Ho richiesto il permesso di soggiorno il 27 marzo scorso. Ho qui la ricevuta. È arrivato/È pronto?

• The police station is where you need to go to report thefts (*furti*), muggings (*scippi*) and other disagreeable events.

My documents/wallet/car have/ has been stolen.	Mi hanno rubato i documenti/ il portafoglio/la macchina.
My bag containing my documents and all my money has been stolen.	Mi hanno rubato la borsetta con i documenti e tutti i soldi.
It happened in the street/on the bus/in the station.	È successo per la strada/in autobus/alla stazione.
I want to report a theft.	Vorrei denunciare un furto.

13 TAKING CARE OF YOUR HEALTH

Parts of the body

arm	braccio
back	schiena
ear	orecchio
eye	occhio
fingers/toes	dita
foot	piede
hand	mano
heart	cuore
intestine	intestino
kidneys	reni
knee	ginocchio
leg	gamba
liver	fegato
lungs	polmoni
mouth	bocca
spine	colonna vertebrale
tongue	lingua
throat	gola
tonsils	tonsille
tooth	dente

Illnesses and symptoms

aids	aids
allergy	allergia
appendicitis	appendicite
asthma	asma

bronchitis/bronchial pneumonia	bronchite/broncopolmonite
chickenpox	varicella
cold	raffreddore
constipation	stitichezza
cystitis	cistite
diarrhoea	diarrea
food poisoning	intossicazione
German measles	rosolia
high blood pressure	pressione alta
infection	infezione
influenza (the 'flu)	influenza
measles	morbillo
mumps	orecchioni
nausea	nausea
scarlet fever	scarlattina
temperature/fever	febbre
vomiting	vomito
whooping cough	pertosse

Types of medicine

(cough) mixture	sciroppo
drops	gocce
eye drops	collirio
gauze	garza
inhalation	inalazione
injection	iniezione
ointment	pomata
pill	pillola/confetto
sleeping pills	sonniferi
suppository	supposta
tablet	pastiglia/compressa

Doctors and specialists

dentist	dentista
dermatologist	dermatologo

ear, nose and throat specialist	**otorino**
family doctor	**medico di base, di famiglia**
gynaecologist	**ginecologo**
heart specialist	**cardiologo**
internist	**internista**
obstetrician	**ostetrico**
optician	**oculista**
orthopaedist	**ortopedico**
pediatrician	**pediatra**
psychiatrist	**psichiatra**
surgeon	**chirurgo**
urologist	**urologo**

HEALTH CARE

The National Health Service (*Servizio Sanitario Nazionale ISSN*) provides free health assistance – or, to be more precise, assistance on payment of the so-called *"ticket"* – to Italian citizens, EEC citizens with the E111 form who are staying temporarily in Europe (this form is obtained from the NHS of the country of origin) and to all foreigners in possession of a work permit. In the cities, the local health centres (*Aziende sanitarie locali/ASL*) have various centres, in different areas of the city, where you have to go to choose and sign on with a doctor. Specialist health care is usually recommended by your doctor, who will write you a prescription for a consultation with a specialist. In the case of an emergency, anyone can go to the casualty department (*Pronto soccorso*) of the nearest hospital. Other public health structures open to everyone also exist in the major cities. These are the *Consultori familiari* or *Consultori pediatrici*, which provide health care and psychological help for families. Besides these, several voluntary associations (*associazioni di volontariato*), both lay and religious, give medical assistance (often specialised assistance) and help (food, washing facilities, clothes, and shelter) to those who are in difficulty.

A. GETTING INFORMATION AND MAKING AN APPOINTMENT

I don't feel well.	**Non mi sento bene/Mi sento poco bene.**
Can you give me the phone number of a good doctor?	**Può darmi il numero di telefono di un buon medico?**

I'd rather see a specialist.	Preferirei consultare uno specialista.
I need a heart specialist.	Ho bisogno di un cardiologo.
Do you know (of) a good gynaecologist?	Conosce/Può consigliarmi un buon ginecologo?
Where's his/her surgery?	Dov'è il suo studio?
What are the surgery hours?	Qual è l'orario delle visite?
Do I need to make an appointment?	Bisogna prendere un appuntamento?
Hello. I'd like to make an (urgent) appointment with the dentist.	Pronto, vorrei fissare un appuntamento (urgente) con il dentista.
When can (s)he see me?	A che ora può ricevermi?
Do I have to pay? Where do I pay?	Devo pagare il ticket? Dove si paga?
I'm ill. Can the doctor come and see me at home before evening?	Sto male. Il dottore può venire a visitarmi a casa prima di sera?

B. AT THE DOCTOR'S

I've got a headache.	Ho mal di testa.
I've hurt my hand.	Mi sono fatto male alla mano.
My knee/back is bad/hurts (a lot).	Mi fa (molto) male il ginocchio/la schiena.
I've got a temperature and I'm aching (all over).	Ho la febbre e mi sento indolenzito.
I'm allergic to antibiotics/aspirin.	Sono allergico agli antibiotici/all'aspirina.
Can I have a medical certificate/prescription for tranquillisers.	Può farmi un certificato medico/la ricetta per un tranquillante?
Where does it hurt?	Dove le fa male?
Has it happened before?	Le è successo altre volte?
What did you eat?	Che cosa ha mangiato?

Please undress.	Si spogli.
Open your mouth. Put out your tongue.	Apra la bocca. Tiri fuori la lingua.
Take a deep breath/Cough!	Faccia un bel respiro/tossisca.
You need to do a blood test/ give a urine/stool sample.	Deve fare l'esame del sangue/ dell'urina/delle feci.
I'll send you to do an x-ray/ (ultrasound) scan.	Le faccio la richiesta di una radiografia/di un'ecografia.

C. AT THE DENTIST'S/GYNAECOLOGIST'S/PEDIATRICIAN'S

I've got really bad toothache in the top/bottom/on the right/left.	Ho un forte mal di denti in alto/in basso/a destra/a sinistra.
I've lost a filling/got tooth decay.	Ho perso l'otturazione/Mi si è cariato un dente.
Could you prescribe me a painkiller?	Può prescrivermi un analgesico?
I think I'm pregnant and I want an abortion.	Temo di essere incinta e vorrei abortire.
I'm two months' pregnant.	Sono incinta di due mesi.
I've got blood spotting/ I often feel nauseous.	Ho delle perdite ematiche/ Ho spesso la nausea.
I'm almost at the end of my pregnancy. From the scan, can you tell me when the baby will be due?	Sono quasi alla fine della gravidanza. Dopo l'ecografia sa dirmi per quando è previsto il parto?
My son fell and hit his head.	Mio figlio è caduto e ha picchiato la testa.
(S)he's got a cough/high temperature.	Ha la tosse/la febbre alta.
Is it infectious?	La malattia è contagiosa?
Can (s)he go to school? Has (s)he to stay in bed?	Può andare a scuola? Deve stare a letto?
I want to vaccinate my child against whooping cough.	Vorrei fare vaccinare mio figlio contro la pertosse.

| How much do I owe you? | Quanto le devo? |
| Can I have a receipt for the insurance? | Posso avere una ricevuta per la mia assicurazione? |

D. AT THE CHEMIST'S

Chemist's shops are easily recognisible by a large flashing green or red cross outside. When the chemist's is shut, a notice in the window indicates where the nearest all-night chemist's in the area is to be found.

Can you tell me where the nearest all-night chemist's is?	Può indicarmi la farmacia di turno più vicina?
I need something for a headache/insect bites.	Ho bisogno di /Mi serve qualcosa contro il mal di testa/le punture di insetti.
Can you give me something for a cough/diarrhoea/burns?	Può darmi una medicina per la tosse/la diarrea/le bruciature?
Can you sell me this antibiotic without a prescription?	Può vendermi questo antibiotico senza ricetta?
Where can I get a prescription at this time?	Dove posso farmi fare una ricetta a quest'ora?
Can't you give me a similar medicine?	Non può darmi un'altra medicina dello stesso tipo?
How often/How long do I have to take these tablets ?	Quante volte al giorno/Per quanti giorni devo prendere queste pastiglie?

E. EMERGENCIES

My wife is injured/has fallen/has hurt herself.	Mia moglie è ferita/è caduta/si è fatta male.
My husband has a weak heart and he's had a heart attack.	Mio marito soffre di cuore e ha avuto un attacco.
Is there a doctor?/Can you get me a doctor?	C'è un medico?/Può chiamarmi un medico?

Where's the hospital/casualty?

Dov'è l'ospedale/il pronto soccorso?

Come quickly! It's serious! There's been an accident.

Presto, è grave! C'è stato un incidente.

I don't feel well. Call a doctor!

Mi sento male. Chiamate un medico!

Call an ambulance immediately. It's urgent!

Fate venire subito un'ambulanza, è urgente!

14 SCHOOL

A. INFORMATION AND ENROLMENTS

Can you tell me who organises Italian language courses for foreigners?

Sa dirmi chi organizza corsi di italiano per stranieri?

Who do I need to see/speak to?

A chi devo rivolgermi?

I'm interested in an evening/ intensive course for adults/ students.

Mi interesserebbe un corso serale/intensivo/per adulti/ per studenti.

What's the address?

Qual è l'indirizzo?

How much does the course/ each lesson cost?

Quanto costa l'iscrizione/ ogni lezione?

How many lessons a week? What times?

Quante lezioni alla settimana? Quali sono gli orari?

When does the next course begin?

Quando comincia il prossimo corso?

When do I need to enrol?

Quando bisogna iscriversi?

What documents do I need?

Quali documenti devo presentare?

Excuse me, which room is the Italian course in?

Scusi, qual è l'aula d'italiano?

I'd like to enrol my son at the creche/nursery school. Are there places free?

Vorrei iscrivere mio figlio all'asilo nido/alla scuola materna. Ci sono posti liberi?

What's the monthly fee? For how many months?

Quanto costa la retta al mese? Per quanti mesi?

How much is the canteen?

Quanto costa la mensa?

What time does school start/ finish?

Qual è l'orario di entrata e di uscita?

B. IN THE CLASSROOM

Come in!/Go out!	**Entrate/Uscite.**
Sit down!/Stand up!	**Sedetevi/Alzatevi.**
Close your exercise books/ Open your books at page 27.	**Chiudete il quaderno/Aprite il libro a pagina 27.**
Listen/Repeat/Answer/Write.	**Ascoltate/Ripetete/Rispondete/ Scrivete.**
Read from the blackboard.	**Leggete sulla lavagna.**
One at a time/All together.	**Uno alla volta/Tutti insieme.**
Work in pairs/groups.	**Lavorate a due a due/a gruppi.**
For tomorrow, study lesson 13 on page 34 and do exercise number 2.	**Per domani studiate la lezione 13 a pagina 34 e fate l'esercizio numero 2.**
Now we'll correct the homework/ exercises together.	**Ora correggiamo insieme i compiti/gli esercizi.**
We'll have lessons from 10 to 12 on Monday/Mondays.	**Lunedì/Il lunedì avremo lezione dalle 10 alle 12.**
Has everyone understood? Any questions?	**Avete capito?/Ci sono domande?**
Excuse me, I don't understand. Could you explain the rule again, please?	**Scusi, non ho capito. Può rispiegare la regola, per favore?**
Where do I have to read?	**Dove devo leggere?**
What do we have to do for next time?	**Che cosa dobbiamo fare per la prossima volta?**
Should we do the exercises? Spoken or written?	**Bisogna fare gli esercizi? Orali o scritti?**
Do we need to learn the dialogue?	**Bisogna imparare il dialogo?**
Excuse me, may I go out/ to the toilet?	**Scusi, posso uscire?/posso andare ai servizi?**

C. SCHOOL RESULTS

Could I speak to Mr Bo?	**Potrei parlare con il professor Bo?**

What time does class II C's Italian/maths teacher see parents?	A che ora riceve il professore di italiano/matematica della classe II C?
I'm... 's mum/dad. S(h)e's in class...	Sono la mamma/il papà di... della classe...
I'd like to know how my son is doing?	Vorrei sapere come va mio figlio.
I'd like to check last month's absences.	Vorrei controllare le assenze dell'ultimo mese.
Could you give me the results of the latest tests/spoken tests?	Può dirmi quali sono i voti delle ultime verifiche/delle ultime interrogazioni?
Does my daughter behave/follow the lessons? Is she too lively?	Mia figlia si comporta bene/segue le lezioni/è troppo vivace?
Are there any problems with your subject?	Ci sono dei problemi nella sua materia?
Has my son made any progress this month/term?	Mio figlio ha fatto dei progressi in questo mese/quadrimestre?
How can I help him?/Should I do something?/What should I do?	Come posso aiutarlo?/Devo intervenire?/Che cosa devo fare?
Please let me know if there are any problems.	La prego di avvisarmi se ci sono difficoltà.
I'll come and speak to you again next month/after the Christmas/Easter holidays.	Tornerò a parlarle il mese prossimo/dopo le vacanze di Natale/di Pasqua.
Thank you for your kindness.	La ringrazio per la sua gentilezza.

15 USING THE PHONE

In Italy you can phone from public phones (phone boxes situated along the road or smaller transparent phone booths) or from bars which have a sign outside showing either a telephone dial on a yellow background or a red telephone receiver.

You will need coins (*monete*) or – more and more frequently – a telephone card (*una scheda telefonica*), which you can buy either in a tobacconist's or at a newsstand.

In the cities there are shops which will let you make international and intercontinental calls at special rates. These shops are often open until late in the evening.

telephone box/booth	**la cabina telefonica**
directory	**l'elenco**
operator	**il/la centralinista**
switchboard	**il centralino**
answering machine	**la segreteria telefonica**
cell phone/mobile	**il (telefono) cellulare**
coins/change	**la moneta**
dialling code	**il prefisso**
free/engaged	**libero/occupato**
line	**la linea**
message	**il messaggio**
public phone	**il telefono pubblico**
telephone call	**la telefonata**
(telephone) card	**la scheda**
telephone number	**il numero di telefono**

EMERGENCY NUMBERS AND USEFUL NUMBERS

112 Carabinieri - Pronto intervento (emergency number)
113 Soccorso pubblico di emergenza (Police-emergency number)
115 Vigili del fuoco - Pronto intervento (Fire Brigade)
116 ACI - Soccorso stradale (Breakdown service)
118 Emergenza sanitaria (Ambulance)
 12 Informazioni elenco abbonati (Directory Enquiries)

A. PUBLIC PHONES

Phoning from a public phone is very straightforward. Just follow the instructions – which are often given in English – inside the phone booth.

FOLLOWING THE INSTRUCTIONS FOR USE

Informazioni e prefissi telefonici	Information and dialling codes
Sganciare il ricevitore e inserire le monete o la carta telefonica	Lift the receiver and insert coins or telephone card
Comporre il numero desiderato	Dial the required number
Digitare il codice utente	Enter user code
Riagganciare e ritirare la carta	Replace receiver and remove phone card
Importo in esaurimento. Inserire altre monete o un'altra scheda	Money running out. Insert coins or another card
Per un'altra telefonata premere il tasto senza riagganciare	To make another phone call press follow-on button without hanging up

Excuse me, I want to make a phone call. Is there a phone near here?	**Scusi, vorrei telefonare. C'è un telefono pubblico qui?**
I'm afraid it's not working.	**Mi dispiace, ma è guasto.**
I'd like a phone card please.	**Vorrei una scheda telefonica.**

How much is that?	Quanto costa?
Can you give me change for 2,000 lire, please?	Può cambiarmi 2000 lire in moneta, per favore?
Excuse me. Could I have the telephone directory?	Per favore, può darmi l'elenco telefonico?
Excuse me. Do you know the code for Genova?	Scusi, sa qual è il prefisso di Genova?
Hello! Is that the information office?	Pronto, è l'ufficio informazioni?
I'd like a number in Pescara – Mr Marco Rossi.	Vorrei il numero telefonico del signor Marco Rossi di Pescara.
Can you call me this number in Aberdeen please?	Può chiamarmi questo numero di Aberdeen?
Do I have to wait long?	C'è molto da aspettare?
How much is it per minute?	Quanto costa la chiamata al minuto?

B. ASKING TO SPEAK TO SOMEONE

Hi Franco. Julie speaking. Can I speak to Luca, please?	Ciao Franco. Sono Julie. Mi passi Luca, per favore?
Ask him to phone me when he gets back.	Gli dici di chiamarmi quando torna?
Is that 02/21338765?	È lo 02/21338765?
Is that Mr Benetti speaking?	Parlo con il signor Benetti?
Good morning. Ann Baker speaking.	Buongiorno. Sono Ann Baker.
Is Mr Bianchi there, please?	C'è il signor Bianchi, per favore?
I'd like to speak to Mrs Ferri, please.	Vorrei parlare con la signora Ferri.
Do you know when (s)he gets back?	Sa quando torna?
Can I leave a message?	Posso lasciare un messaggio?
What time can I call back?	A che ora posso richiamarla?

Could you get him/her to call me back at this number?	Potrebbe farmi richiamare a questo numero?
Can I speak to someone else?	Posso parlare con qualcun altro?
Who do I need to contact for information?.	A chi devo rivolgermi per avere delle informazioni?
Thank you for your help.	La ringrazio della sua cortesia.
Goodbye and thank you again.	Arrivederla e grazie ancora.

C. REPLYING

Hello!	Pronto.
Luca's not in. Shall I get him to call you back?	Luca non c'è. Ti faccio richiamare?
If you like, I can leave him a message.	Se vuoi, posso lasciargli un appunto.
Hullo! Pat Fisher speaking.	Pronto. Qui Pat Fisher.
Alpex. Good morning.	Società Alpex buongiorno.
Who's speaking, please?	Chi parla, per favore?
Who would you like to speak to?	Con chi desidera parlare?
One moment, please. I'll put you through.	Un momento, prego. Glielo passo subito.
Hold on, please.	Resti in linea/Attenda.
I'm afraid he's not here.	Mi dispiace, non c'è.
Would you like to call back later or leave a message?	Vuole richiamare più tardi o preferisce lasciare un messaggio?

D. PROBLEMS ON THE PHONE

To report problems with the phone → **10. Domestic problems**: A. Utilities.

It's always engaged.	È sempre occupato.
You've got the wrong number. This is 06/98346711.	Ha sbagliato numero. Qui è lo 06/98346711.

I'm so sorry.	Scusi tanto.
Sorry, what did you say?	Scusi, come ha detto?
I'm sorry, I don't understand.	Mi dispiace, non capisco.
I'm not Italian. Could you speak a bit slower?	Non sono italiano, può parlare più lentamente?
Hello! Can you hear me? I can hardly hear you.	Pronto, mi sente? Io la sento malissimo.
Can you speak up a bit?	Può parlare a voce più alta?
There's a lot of interference (on the line).	La linea è disturbata.
I can't hear you. Could you call me back?	Non sento niente. Può richiamare, per favore?
I'll hang up and try again.	Riattacco e rifaccio il numero.
We were cut off.	È caduta la linea.

16 READING AND UNDERSTANDING INSTRUCTIONS

A. ROAD SIGNS

area di servizio	Service station
centro città	City centre
corsia di emergenza	Emergency lane
curva pericolosa	Dangerous bend
deviazione	Diversion
divieto di sorpasso/di sosta	No overtaking/parking
lavori in corso	Road works
pagamento pedaggio	(Motorway)Toll
parcheggio (a pagamento)	(Pay) Car park
passaggio pedonale	Zebra crossing
polizia stradale	Traffic police
rallentare	Slow down
tangenziale	Ring road
traffico rallentato	Slow traffic
vigili urbani	Traffic wardens
zona disco	Disc zone
zona pedonale	Pedestrian zone

B. SIGNS AND NOTICES

affittasi	To let/rent
arrivi	Arrivals
attenti al cane	Beware of the dog!
avanti!	Come in!

biglietteria	Ticket office
camere (in affitto)	Room to rent
cassa	Cash desk
chiuso per ferie	Closed for holidays
entrata	Entrance
entrata libera	Free entrance
esaurito	Sold out
fumatori	Smokers
fuori servizio	Out of order
informazioni	Information
partenze	Departures
privato	Private
riservato	Reserved
saldi	Sales
sconto	Reduction
tirare/spingere	Pull/Push
toilette(s)/W.C.	Toilet
uscita	Exit
uscita di sicurezza	Emergency exit
vendesi	For sale
vietato fumare	No smoking
vietato l'ingresso	No entrance

C. INSTRUCTIONS FOR CASHPOINTS

Inserire la carta	Insert card
Digitare il codice segreto	Enter PIN
Cancella dato	Cancel
Conferma dato	Confirm
Esegui	Enter
Prelievo	Withdrawal
Versamento	Payment
Saldo	Balance

Operazione in corso	Wait
Annulla operazione	Cancel operation
Vuoi lo scontrino?	With/without a receipt?
Ritira la carta/i soldi/lo scontrino entro ... secondi	Take the card/money/receipt within ... seconds.

D. ELECTRICAL HOUSEHOLD APPLIANCES

accendere/spegnere	switch on/off
allacciamento	connection (gas, phone)
avvitare/svitare	screw/unscrew
batteria (ricaricabile)	(rechargeable) battery
caratteristiche tecniche	technical characteristics
cartolina di garanzia	guarantee card
collegare/scollegare l'apparecchio	connect/disconnect the appliance
danno	damage
garanzia	guarantee
guasto	failure/something wrong
inserire/disinserire la spina	plug in/disconnect the plug
interruttore	switch
manutenzione	maintenance
pila (elettrica)	torch
pile	batteries
precauzioni d'uso	safety precautions
presa di corrente, presa elettrica	socket/outlet
programmare	programme
pulizia	cleaning
pulsante/tasto	button
reclamo	complaint/claim
scomparto batterie	battery compartment
spia (luminosa)	warning light
spina	(electric) plug
togliere/mettere il coperchio	take off/put on the cover/top
voltaggio	voltage

E. INSTRUCTIONS FOR TAKING MEDICINES

A digiuno/A stomaco pieno	On an empty/full stomach
Agitare prima dell'uso	Shake before using
Composizione	Active ingredients
Conservare al riparo dalla luce/dall'umidità/a temperature inferiori a...	Keep away from light/damp/temperatures less than...
Consultare il medico in caso di...	Consult a doctor in the case of...
Effetti collaterali	Side effects
Leggere attentamente le avvertenze	Read the instructions carefully
Modalità d'uso	Instructions for use
Non superare le dosi consigliate/Rispettare le dosi prescritte	Do not exceed the stated dose
Per uso interno/esterno	For internal/external use only
Posologia: una compressa tre volte al dì/ogni otto ore	Dosage: one tablet three times a day/every eight hours
Precauzioni	Precautions
Prima/Dopo i pasti	Before/After meals
Rivolgersi al proprio medico	Consult your doctor
Scadenza	Expiry date
Sovradosaggio	Overdose
Tenere il medicinale fuori dalla portata dei bambini	Keep medicines out of reach of children
Venduto dietro presentazione di ricetta medica	Sold by prescription only

17 WRITING

Even if phoning is fast and very practical, on some occasions it is important to know how to send a brief written message.

A. GREETINGS CARDS

• In Italy it is still usual to send greetings cards – printed or hand-written – to friends and acquaintances at Christmas (*Natale*) and New Year (*Capodanno*).

Un affettuoso augurio di Buone Feste a te e alla tua famiglia.	With warmest Christmas greetings to you and your family.
I miei più cari auguri/Con i migliori auguri di Buon Natale e di un felice Anno Nuovo.	My very best wishes/With best wishes for a merry Christmas and a happy New Year.
Sinceri auguri per un felice Natale e un bellissimo 2003.	Best wishes for a happy Christmas and a wonderful 2003.
Auguro a Lei e alla Sua famiglia un lieto Natale e un Nuovo Anno prospero e sereno.	Wishing you and your family a merry Christmas and a happy and prosperous New Year.

• On occasions such as birthdays, weddings and Christmas, it is a nice idea to send a written greeting along with a present or a bunch of flowers.

Tanti auguri per il tuo compleanno!	Best wishes on your birthday!
Con tanto affetto e gli auguri più sinceri.	With lots of love and sincere best wishes.
Viva gli sposi! Con l'augurio di una lunga e felice vita insieme.	Congratulations to the newlyweds! With best wishes for a long and happy life together.

Alla cara Eleonora con tutto il
nostro affetto.

To dear Eleonora with all our
love.

B. POSTCARDS

A few words written on a postcard – to say hello, to stay in touch,
to give news of yourself – are always nice to get.

Ciao a tutti da Ann e Bill.

Hullo to everyone from Ann
and Bill.

Saluti da Palermo.

Greetings from Palermo.

Un caro/affettuoso saluto per
ricordare i bei momenti passati
insieme.

Fondest greetings to remember
good times spent together.

Vi ricordo con affetto.

Thinking of you. With love,

Sono arrivato bene e comincio a
conoscere la città. Scriverò presto.

I got here fine and I'm getting to
know (my way round) the city.
I'll write soon.

Non vi ho dimenticato e sto bene.
E voi? Cercherò di telefonarvi
appena possibile.

I haven't forgotten you! I'm fine,
and you? I'll try to phone as
soon as I can.

C. SHORT MESSAGES

If you need to ask a favour (*chiedere una cortesia*) or thank someone (*ringraziare*) for their kindness, one quick and practical way is
to write a short message on a plain white card.

Can I ask you a favour?

Posso chiederle una cortesia?

Would you mind doing me a
favour?

Le dispiacerebbe farmi un favore?

Can I ask you to...?

Posso chiederle di...?

Excuse me, could you...?

Mi scusi, potrebbe...?

Thanks very much.

Con mille ringraziamenti.

Heartfelt thanks.

La ringrazio di cuore.

Thanking you in advance for
your patience.

La ringrazio anticipatamente della
sua pazienza.

Thank you so much for your kindness.	Grazie infinite per la cortesia.
Would you mind collecting a parcel for me? It should arrive this afternoon.	Le dispiacerebbe ritirarmi un pacco che dovrebbe arrivare oggi nel pomeriggio?
Thank you very much for your kind hospitality and for the friendship you've shown me.	Grazie infinite per la cordialità della vostra accoglienza e per l'amicizia che mi avete dimostrato.
I'm writing to thank you once more for your kind hospitality.	Le scrivo per ringraziarla ancora della sua cortese ospitalità.
Thank you very much for your help. We are very grateful.	Le siamo molto grati per il suo interessamento e la ringraziamo di cuore.

D. WRITING LETTERS

Drafting a letter in Italian follows fairly precise rules, especially if the letter is a formal one addressed to someone you do not know (*lettera formale*) or to someone in an office (*lettera commerciale*). The letter should be typed and you must remember to use the more formal **Lei** form when writing (→ **4. Personal relations**: A. Addressing people). When drafting the letter you need to pay particular attention to syntax and respect the rules for layout and paragraphing.

Informal letters (*lettere confidenziali*), on the other hand, can be handwritten (*scritte a mano*), provided they are easily legible. Informal letters are structured more freely and certain parts of the letter – for example the sender's name – can be missed out. The language is simpler and more direct and the familiar form (*tu*) is used.

Drafting a formal or business letter

• Town/city and date (*Luogo e data*). These are written in the top right-hand corner or at the end of the letter in the bottom left-hand corner. Begin with the city – followed by a comma – then day, month and year.

• If you are not using headed paper, the address of the person who is writing (*il mittente*) is written in the top left-hand corner. Begin with name and surname, then the street and number and, finally, the post code and town.

• The addressee (*il destinatario*) – the person to whom the letter is addressed – is written a few lines below that of the sender, on the right-hand side. Begin with name and surname, then the street and number and, finally, the post code and town. The adjective **Spettabile** is always written in front of company names.

• When writing formal letters you begin with the formula **Egregi signori** (**Dear Sirs**) or **Egregio signore/Gentile signora** (**Dear Sir/Madam**) or **Egregio signor.../Gentile signora...** (**Dear Mr/Mrs...**) followed by the surname. In informal letters **Dear** (*Caro /Cara*) followed by the first name is used.

• On the following line you begin the real letter using a small and not a capital letter to begin with. The exception to this rule is when you begin with the polite **Vi** (**You**) as in "*Vi informo*"/"I am writing to inform you". Divide your letter into three paragraphs: introduction, content and conclusion.

• End the letter with a closing phrase (*frase finale di saluto*), which will vary according to the relationship you have with the other person.

• End a formal/business letter with one of the following accepted phrases:

Distinti saluti.	Best regards,
La prego di gradire i miei migliori/ più cordiali saluti.	Please accept my best regards,
Con i migliori saluti.	With my best regards,
Un cortese/cordiale saluto.	Kind regards,
Cordialmente.	Yours sincerely,

• End an informal letter with a more affectionate phrase:

Ciao.	Bye,
A presto.	See you soon/Hear from you soon,
Affettuosi saluti / Un caro saluto.	All the best/Love and hugs,

• You should always sign a letter by hand (*a mano*) on the bottom right-hand side of the page. If it is a formal letter it is better to leave a space for your signature (*firma*) and then type your name underneath for clarity.

Milano, 5 marzo 2002

Paul Smith
Corso Garibaldi 109
20100 Milano

Spettabile
Credito Italiano
Viale Molise 12
20100 Milano

Egregi signori,

con la presente Vi comunico che trasferirò la mia residenza in Piazza
Lodi 27, 20100 Milano.

Vi prego di inviare la corrispondenza al nuovo indirizzo a partire dal
15 maggio prossimo.

Distinti saluti.

Paul Smith

Milano, 5 March 2002

Paul Smith
Corso Garibaldi 109
20100 Milano

Spettabile
Credito Italiano
Viale Molise 12
20100 Milano

Dear Sirs,

I am writing to inform you that I will be transferring my residence
to Piazza Lodi 27, 20100 Milano.

Please will you send any correspondence to my new address as
from 15th May.

Yours faithfully,

Paul Smith

Roma, 2 ottobre 2003

Michael Amis
Piazza Adriano 18
10035 Roma

Spettabile
Assicurazione Sicurmed
Via Pistoia 12
10037 Roma

Egregi signori,
Vi informo con la presente che la mia auto Fiat Uno targata Roma
AZ3287TR di colore blu assicurata presso la Vostra compagnia
(polizza n. 99876588) è stata rubata ieri tra le 17 e le 20. L'auto era
stata regolarmene parcheggiata, con le portiere chiuse a chiave e
l'antifurto inserito, in via Pantano all'altezza del numero 50.
Ho sporto regolare denuncia al commissariato di zona e allego copia
del documento rilasciatomi.
Resto in attesa di Vostre comunicazioni e saluto distintamente.

Allegato
Copia denuncia

Michael Amis

Roma, 2 October 2003

Michael Amis
Piazza Adriano 18
10035 Roma

Spettabile
Assicurazione Sicurmed
Via Pistoia 12
10037 Roma

Dear Sirs,
I am writing to inform you that my car, a blue Fiat Uno with a
Rome numberplate AZ3287TR, which is insured with your company
(policy no. 99876588) was stolen yesterday between 17.00 and
20.00. The car was legally parked outside Via Pantano, 50 . It was
locked and the antitheft alarm was on.
I reported the theft at the police station and enclose a copy of the
documents given to me.
I look forward to receiving a reply from you.
Yours faithfully,

Michael Amis

Enclosed
Copy of police report

E. CURRICULUM VITAE/CV

Anyone looking for work should prepare a curriculum vitae (or CV) which gives information regarding educational background (*formazione scolastica*) and previous work experience (*precedenti esperienze di lavoro*) at a glance.

This information should be presented in a clear, concise way, chronologically listing the main, professional experience of the candidate, and emphasising the most positive and interesting details. For example, you should point out if you speak any foreign languages or possess a driving licence, if you are willing to begin work immediately or are willing to travel or change work location.

Anyone who is looking for their first job and is without previous work experience should emphasise any personal characteristics (for example willingness to work, reliability, honesty, dynamism and perseverance) which will inspire trust in them.

It is best to send a brief accompanying letter with the CV in which you state where you saw the job advertised.

MODEL CV

Cognome	Krishen
Nome	Pradip
Indirizzo	Via Garibaldi 288 – 30100 Venezia Mestre
Telefono	041/33981671
Luogo e data di nascita	Calcutta, India 4/12/1975
Nazionalità	indiana
Stato civile	celibe
Servizio militare	assolto
Studi	licenza di studi professionali conseguita nel 1990 a Bombay, India
Lingue	inglese ottimo
	italiano buono
	francese discreto
Esperienze	5 anni come operaio addetto alla catena di montaggio presso un'azienda metalmeccanica in Medio Oriente
	da 5 anni in Italia
	2 anni come operaio specializzato presso un'azienda automobilistica del nord Italia

disponibilità immediata
attitudine e buona volontà a imparare
patente internazionale

Surname	Krishen
Name	Pradip
Address	Via Garibaldi 288 – 30100 Venezia Mestre
Telephone	041/33981671
Place and date of birth	Calcutta, India 4/12/1975
Nationality	Indian
Marital status	Single
Military service	completed
Qualifications	Technical college diploma (1990), Bombay, India
Languages	English: fluent
	Italian: proficient
	French: competent
Professional experience	5 years as production line worker for a metalworking company in the Middle East
	Five years in Italy
	Two years as specialised worker for an automobile company in north Italy
	Available immediately
	Able and willing to learn
	International driving licence

18 CLASSIFIED ADVERTISEMENTS

The major daily and local newspapers publish a large number of advertisements – subdivided into categories – in the pages reserved for classified advertisements (*Annunci*). In most large towns there are also weekly papers which specialise in publishing free advertisements for jobs, accomodation, household goods, cars, work equipment and sports gear etc.

It is not always easy to understand these advertisements, however, as they are usually written without punctuation, in abbreviated form, using idioms and specific terminology (*termini specifici*) which can render them almost incomprehensible to non-Italians.

A. JOBS

If you are looking for work you should read the relevant sections entitled: *Offerte di lavoro/Lavoro: Offerte/Ricerche di collaboratori* (Job vacancies/Situations vacant). You can also pay to have a classified ad. inserted in the section *Richieste di lavoro/Offerte di collaborazione* (Positions sought) . For information and useful job vocabulary → **8.Looking for work**.

assistenza anziani	companion (for elderly people)
assumere	take on (somebody)
automunito	own transport provided
autosufficienti e non	(not) self-sufficient
baby-sitting	baby-sitting
cercasi	look for
colf (collaboratrice domestica)	domestic help (person)
collaborazioni domestiche	home help (job)
CV	CV
dinamico	dynamic

disponibilità immediata	available immediately
...enne (30enne/23enne ecc.)	...years old (e.g. 30/23 years old)
esperienza	experience
libero subito	available immediately
max.	maximum (of)
militassolto/militesente	not required to do military service
motivato	motivated
multinazionale	multinational
patente/patentato	driving licence/with a current driving licence
qualificato	qualified
referenziato	with references
ricercare	look for
società immobiliare	real estate
spese escluse	exclusive of costs
tempo parziale	part-time
tempo pieno	full time
vitto e alloggio	board and lodging

Job vacancies/situations vacant

Coppia con bambino cerca colf seria, dinamica, esperienza. Telefonare per appuntamento.

Serious, dynamic and experienced home help wanted for couple with baby. Phone for an appointment.

Società di servizi cerca operai max. 30enni per lavoro magazzinieri full o part-time. Presentarsi con CV aggiornato.

Services company looking for warehousemen, full or part-time. Max. age 30. Applicants must have updated CV.

Società immobiliare Ancona assume impiegato/a contabilità disponibile, motivato/a, buona conoscenza lingua inglese.

Real estate company, Ancona, has a vacancy for a motivated accounts clerk. Available immediately. Good knowledge of English required.

Cerchiamo cameriere, camerieri, cuochi per nuovo ristorante Genova. Inviare CV con foto a ...

Waiters, waitresses and chefs required for newly-opened restaurant in Genova. Send CV with photo to ...

Positions sought

Giovane filippino serio referenziato cerca collaborazione domestica baby-sitter, assistenza anziani autosufficienti e non. Disponibilità immediata.	Young, reliable Filipino looking for position as home help, baby-sitter or companion for elderly person (self-sufficient or not). Available immediately. References available.
Egiziano 22enne patente esperienza cerca lavoro tempo pieno o parziale: aiuto magazziniere, autista, fattorino o altro.	22-year-old Egyptian looking for full-time/part-time work as assistant storeman, driver, deliveryman etc. Experienced. Current driving licence.

B. PROPERTY

The real estate sections (*Immobili /Immobiliare*) advertise flats for sale and flats or rooms to rent. They are divided zone by zone in the cities for easier reference. For useful phrases and terminology regarding accomodation → **9. Looking for accomodation**.

accessoriato	fully equipped
adiacenze	vicinity
affare	bargain
affittare	(to) rent
affittasi	(to) let/rent
affitto	rent
angolo cottura	cooking area
appartamento signorile/di lusso	luxury flat
aria condizionata	air conditioning
arredato/ammobiliato	furnished
bilocale/trilocale	two-roomed/three-roomed flat
buono/ottimo stato	good/excellent condition
completamente ristrutturato	fully renovated
con/senza ascensore	with/without lift
cucinino	kitchenette
doppi servizi	two bathrooms
libero/occupato	empty/occupied
monolocale	one-roomed flat

mq/m²	square metre(s)/m²
palazzo recente/d'epoca	new/historic building
piano	floor
piano terra	ground floor
prezzo ragionevole/interessante	fair/interesting price
privato	private
riscaldamento centralizzato	centralised heating
ristrutturare	to renovate
completamente ristrutturato	fully renovated
soleggiato	sunny
spese comprese/escluse	inclusive/exclusive of costs/charges
trattabili	negotiable
vendesi	for sale
vendita/in vendita	sale/for sale
vista su	looks onto…
vuoto	empty

For Sale

Affare! Monolocale 32 mq 3° piano senza ascensore cucinino ristrutturato balcone cantina. Prezzo interessante.

Bargain! Renovated one-roomed flat (32 m²) with kitchenette, balcony and cellar. 3rd floor without lift. Interesting price.

To Let/Rent

Monolocale vuoto interamente ristrutturato cucinino bagno affitto solo privati.

Fully renovated one-roomed flat with kitchenette and bathroom. Empty. Private rental only.

Bellissimo bilocale sesto piano luminoso tranquillo affittasi L. 1.200.000 spese escluse.

Beautiful two-roomed flat, sixth floor. Gets plenty of light, quiet. Rent L. 1,200,000 exclusive of charges.

Furnished bedsits to rent

Zona stazione centrale adiacenze metropolitana monolocale arredato ogni comodità.

Central Station area, metro nearby. Furnished bedsitter with all mod cons.

Monolocale ristrutturato tranquillo cucinino doccia affittasi zona fiera.

Newly renovated bedsit to rent. Kitchenette and shower. Quiet. Fiera area.

C. SUNDRY

Ford Fiesta rossa anno 1997 43.000 km ottimo stato vendo 7 milioni (trattabili).

'97 Red Ford Fiesta. 43,000 km. Excellent condition. Selling for 7 million (negotiable).

Vendo lavatrice Candy 3 anni ottimo stato prezzo modico.

For sale. Candy washing machine, 3 years old, excellent condition, good price.

Privato acquisterebbe automobile piccola cilindrata marmitta catalitica buono stato chilometraggio e prezzo ragionevoli.

Private buyer looking for car: small engine, catalytic converter, good condition, low mileage, reasonable price.

Cerco frigorifero con freezer qualsiasi marca buono stato.

Fridge-freezer wanted in good condition. Any brand.

PART TWO

GRAMMAR

1. SENTENCE FORMATION

A. Affirmative sentences

• Word order in Italian is not as rigid as in English. However, you often begin with the **subject**.

Il pane è sul tavolo.   The bread is on the table.

• All verbs must have a subject in English whereas in Italian the subject can be – and often is – omitted because the verb ending gives you this information.

Arrivo verso le sette/   I'll arrive towards seven/
Arriviamo verso le sette.   We'll arrive towards seven.

• In Italian the subject pronoun is often used for **emphasis**.

Io lavoro e **tu** non fai niente!   I work and you do nothing!

B. Interrogative sentences

In spoken Italian it is sufficient to use **intonation** to form a question. In written Italian just add a **question mark** at the end of the sentence. The word order is fairly flexible.

Sei italiano?   Are you Italian?

È arrivato tuo fratello?/   Has your brother arrived?
Tuo fratello è arrivato?

C. Negative sentences

To make a sentence negative simply put **_non_** in front of the verb.

Maria non vuole venire.   Maria doesn't want to come.

Non gridare!   Don't shout!

2. GENDER FORMS

Italian has two gender forms: **masculine** and **feminine**. In the case of people and animals, the two gender forms usually correspond to **male** and **female**.

il figlio/la figlia	son/daughter
il commesso/la commessa	shop assistant (man)/ shop assistant (woman)
il gatto/la gatta	cat (male)/cat (female)

3. ARTICLES

In Italian the article **agrees with** its noun. It can therefore be masculine or feminine, singular or plural.

la città (f./sing.)	the city
un uomo (m./sing.)	a man
le donne (f./pl.)	women
gli amici (m./pl.)	friends

A. Definite article

The definite article is used before nouns to refer to someone or something already mentioned previously and to refer to someone or something **specific**.

È **il** vocabolario d'inglese usato da mio padre.	It's the English dictionary my father used.

Forms

- *il* masculine singular

il latte	the milk

- *lo* masculine singular before *gn*, *pn*, *ps*, *s* + **consonant** and *z*

lo psicologo	the psychologist
lo stadio	the stadium
lo zucchero	the sugar

- *la* feminine singular

  la donna   the woman

- *l'* before masculine and feminine nouns which begin with a **vowel** (*a*, *e*, *i*, *o*, *u*)

  l'amica   the friend
  l'uomo   the man

- *i* masculine plural

  i bambini   the children

- *gli* masculine plural before **vowels**, *gn*, *pn*, *ps*, *s* + **consonant** and *z*

  gli orologi   the clocks/watches
  gli zii   aunt and uncle/uncles

- *le* feminine plural

  le ragazze   the girls

B. Indefinite article

The indefinite article is used only with **singular** nouns to make **general** statements.

Forms

- *un* masculine

  un lavoro   a job

- *uno* masculine before *gn*, *pn*, *ps*, *s* + **consonant** and *z*

  uno specchio   a mirror
  uno zio   an uncle

- *una* feminine

  una casa   a house

- *un'* feminine before vowels

  un'amica   a friend (f.)

C. Quantifiers

The quantifiers **some** and **any** are used to express **a certain amount**, not a precise amount. In Italian, unlike in English, these quantifiers can be omitted, especially if the sentence is negative. For example: "I have**n't any** friends" would simply be translated as "***Non*** *ho amici*".

Forms

- ***del/dello/dell'*** masculine singular

  del pane/dello zucchero/   some bread/sugar/vinegar
  dell'aceto

- ***della/dell'*** feminine singular

  della salsa/dell'insalata   some sauce/salad

- ***dei/degli*** masculine plural

  dei colleghi/degli amici   some colleagues/friends

- ***delle*** feminine plural

  delle donne   some women

4. NOUNS AND THEIR PLURALS

- Nouns which end in **-o** are usually **masculine**. The plural is formed by eliminating the **-o** and adding **-i**.

il letto → **i** lett**i**   bed → beds

- Some frequently used words ending in **-o** are, however, **feminine** and **remain the same** in the plural.

l'auto/**la** moto/**la** foto → **le** auto/**le** moto/**le** foto
car/motorbike/photo → cars/motor bikes/photos

- Nouns ending in **-a** are usually **feminine.** The plural is formed by eliminating the **-a** and adding **-e**. However, if the noun is **masculine**, add **-i**.

la camera → **le** camere (f.)   room → rooms

l'artista → **gli** artisti (m.)   artist → artists

• Nouns ending in **-e** can be masculine or feminine. The plural is formed by eliminating the **-e** and adding **-i**. Those which end in **-i** and **-u** remain the same.

il signore → **i** signori	gentleman → gentlemen
la notte → **le** notti	night → nights
l'analisi → **le** analisi	analysis → analyses

• Nouns ending in **-co**, **-ca**, **-go**, **-ga** take the following plural forms **-chi**, **-che**, **-ghi**, **-ghe**.

il parco → **i** parchi	park → parks
l'amica → **le** amiche	friend → friends
il collega → **i** colleghi	colleague → colleagues

• Be careful with exceptions:

l'amico → **gli** amici	friend→ friends
il medico → **i** medici	doctor → doctors

5. ADJECTIVES

Adjectives agree with their noun in Italian:

un libro caro	an expensive book
una rivista cara	an expensive magazine

They usually come after the noun but can come before it. To make adjectives plural, follow the rules for nouns → **4. Nouns and their plurals**.
As nouns referring to people and animals have both a feminine and a masculine form, adjective agreement follows one of the two following rules:

• the adjective ends in **-o** if the noun is masculine but ends in **-a** if the noun is feminine

un uomo alto/**una** donna alta	a tall man/a tall woman

• adjectives ending in **-e** remain the same both in the masculine and in the feminine

un bambino/**una** bambina vivac**e**

a lively baby/child

A. Comparisons

• To form a comparative in Italian put **più** (more) or **meno** (less/not as...as) before the adjective.

Il mio appartamento è **più/meno** caro **del** tuo.

My flat is more/less expensive than yours.

Il mio appartamento è **meno** caro **del** tuo.

My flat is not as expensive as yours.

• To say that something is equal to something else in Italian use **come** (the same as/as... as).

Questa macchina costa **come** quella.

This car costs the same as that one.

• To form a superlative in Italian put **il più** (the most) or **il meno** (the least) before the adjective.

Questi appartamenti sono **i più/i meno** cari.

These flats are the most/the least expensive.

B. Intensifying adjectives

If you want to intensify the effect of what you are saying, you can put **molto** (very) in front of an adjective or substitute the final letter of the adjective with **-issimo**, which corresponds to an intensifying adjective (e.g. *cattivissimo*/terrible) in English.

È bello → È **molto** bello/bell**issimo**

It's nice → It's very nice/wonderful

Questa pizza è buona → **molto** buona/buon**issima** (**ottima**).

This pizza is good → very good/excellent

6. PERSONAL PRONOUNS

A. Subject pronouns

Io	I
Tu	You
Egli/lui	He
Ella/lei	She
Esso/a	It
Noi	We
Voi	You (pl.)
Essi	They (m.)
Esse	They (f.)

B. Object pronouns

	Before the verb	After a preposition
Io	mi	me
Tu	ti	te
Lui	lo/gli	lui (m.)
Lei	la/le	lei (f.)
esso/a	lo/la	esso/a
Noi	ci	noi
Voi	vi	voi
Essi	li	loro (m.)
Esse	le	loro (f.)

Mi ha invitata.	He/She invited me.
Ti ho visto	I saw you.
Lo/la vedo stasera.	I'm seeing him/her this evening.
Gli/le hai telefonato?	Did you phone him/her?
Ci avvisi?	Will you let us know?
Li/Le ho avvisati/e.	I let them know.
Vieni con **me**?/con **noi**?	Are you coming with me/with us?
L'ho fatto per **te/lui/voi**.	I did it for you/him/you. (pl.)
Sono uscita con **lui/lei/loro**.	I went out/left with him/her/them.

- With **infinitive** verbs the pronoun merges with the verb.

Non posso **farlo**. (fare + lo)   I can't do it.

7. POSSESSIVE FORMS

In Italian, unlike in English, the possessive adjective and possessive pronoun have the same form. The possessive adjective is **usually** preceded by the article in Italian, whereas the pronoun is **always** preceded by the article. In the table below the possessive adjective (my, your etc.) comes first; the possessive pronoun (mine, yours etc.) comes afterwards. N.B. Possessive adjectives and pronouns agree with their noun in Italian.

	Singular		Plural	
Masculine	il mio	my/mine	i miei	my/mine
	il tuo	your/yours	i tuoi	your/yours
	il suo	his/his	i suoi	his/his
	il nostro	our/ours	i nostri	our/ours
	il vostro	your/yours	i vostri	your/yours
	il loro	their/theirs	i loro	their/theirs
Feminine	la mia	my/mine	le mie	my/mine
	la tua	your/yours	le tue	your/yours
	la sua	her/hers	le sue	her/hers
	la nostra	our/ours	le nostre	our/ours
	la vostra	your/yours	le vostre	your/yours
	la loro	their/theirs	le loro	their/theirs

Il mio bambino/**Mio** figlio è alla materna. E **il tuo**?

My child/son is at nursery school. And yours?

Dov'è **il suo** libro d'italiano?

Where is his/her Italian book?

Se **la vostra** macchina non parte, prendete **la nostra**.

If your car won't start, take ours.

Non trova più **le sue** cose.

He/She can't find his/her things any more.

La mia casa non è lontana.

My house isn't very far.

Il suo lavoro è interessante, **il mio** noioso.

His/her work is interesting. Mine is boring.

8. DEMONSTRATIVE

There are two forms in Italian: **questo** (this) which refers to things near the speaker, or near in terms of time and **quello** (that) which refers to things further from the speaker or more distant in terms of time. These can be either adjectives or pronouns.

	Singular		Plural	
Masculine	questo/quest'	this	questi	these
	quel/quello/quell'	that	quelli	those
Feminine	questa /quest'	this	queste	these
	quella/quell'	that	quelle	those

Questo letto/**Quest'**armadio è troppo piccolo.	This bed/This wardrobe is too small.
Dammi **quel** giornale, per favore. No, **quell'**altro.	Give me that newspaper, please. No, that other one.
Non voglio **questa**, voglio **quella**.	I don't want this one. I want that one.
Vuoi un po' di **questo**?	Do you want a little of this?
Questa primavera/ **Quest'**estate andrò a casa.	I'll go home this spring/ this summer.
Quell'anno ero a Parigi.	I was in Paris that year.

9. INDEFINITE ADJECTIVES AND PRONOUNS

Those most used in Italian are:

nessuno/a	nobody/no one/not... anyone
niente	nothing/not... anything
alcuni/e (pl.)	a few
qualche (sing.)	some
qualcuno/a	somebody/someone
ogni (invar.)	each/every
altro/a/i/e	other(s)
tutto/a/i/e	all/everybody/everyone

Non ho visto **nessuno/niente**.	I didn't see anyone/anything
L'ho sentito **alcuni** giorni fa/ **qualche** giorno fa.	I heard from him a few days ago.
Ha telefonato **qualcuno**?	Did anyone phone?
Telefona **ogni** giorno.	He/She phones every day.
Dove sono gli **altri**?	Where are the others?
Tutti lo sanno.	Everyone knows.

10. RELATIVE PRONOUNS

Many different relative pronouns exist in Italian. The easiest one to use is *che* because you can never go wrong! *Che* is used for masculine and feminine, singular and plural. After a preposition it becomes *cui*.

La ragazza **che** parla con Carlo.	The girl who is talking to Carlo.
I colleghi **che** lo accompagnano.	The colleagues who are with him.
Il film di **cui** parlate mi è piaciuto.	I liked the film (that) you are talking about.

11. INTERROGATIVES

A. Interrogative adjectives

The interrogative adjectives are *quale* and *che*. *Che* is also used in exclamations.

Che ore sono?	What time is it?
Che/quale film hai scelto?	Which film have you chosen?
Che bel bambino!	What a lovely baby!

B. Interrogative pronouns

The interrogative pronoun *chi* refers to people whereas *che cosa* refers to things.

| **Chi** vuole venire? | Who wants to come? |

A **chi** hai telefonato?	Who did you phone?
Con **chi** lavori?	Who do you work with?
Che cosa hai detto?	What did you say?

C. Other interrogative forms

Other words which are useful if you want to ask questions are **perché**, **quanto**, **quando** and **come**.

Perché non rispondi?	Why don't you reply?
Quanto costa?	How much does it cost?
Quando verrai?	When are you coming?
Come hai fatto?	How did you do it?

12. PREPOSITIONS

a	to
con	with
da	from/to
di	of
dopo	after
fra	between/in (time)
in	in
per	for
prima di	before
sopra	on /above/over
sotto	below/under
su	on
tra	between

Sono andato **a** Milano.	I went to Milano.
Lavoro **con** Francesca.	I work with Francesca.
Vengo **da** Bologna e vado **a** Torino.	I've come from Bologna and I'm going to Torino
Verrai anche tu **da** Anna?	Are you going to go to Anna's, too?

Questo giocattolo è fatto **di** legno.	This toy is made of wood.
Ci vediamo **fra** qualche minuto.	See you in a few minutes.
Ci vediamo **prima di/dopo** cena.	See you before/after dinner.
In estate fa troppo caldo.	It's too hot in summer.
I fiori sono **per** te.	The flowers are for you.
La borsa è **sopra/sotto** la sedia.	The bag is on/under the chair.
Tra/Fra me e lui non ci sono problemi.	There are no problems between us.

- The prepositions *di*, *a*, *da*, *in*, *su* merge **with the article** of the word which follows them.

Il nome **del** posto/**della** città.	The name of the place/city.
Parlane **agli** altri/**alle** altre.	Speak to the others.
È caduto **dalla** scala/**dal** tetto.	He fell off the ladder/roof.
Ho 20.000 lire **nel** portafoglio/**nella** borsa.	I've got 20,000 lire in my wallet/bag.
C'è un libro **sul** tavolo/**sullo** sgabello.	There's a book on the table/stool.

13. VERBS

In Italian verbs can be:

- **transitive** (having or needing an object). No preposition is required before the object.

Ho mangiato una mela.	I ate an apple.
Abbiamo comprato una televisione nuova.	We (have) bought a new TV.

- or **intransitive** (not followed by a direct object). If followed by an indirect object a preposition is usually necessary.

Devi telefonare **a** tua sorella.	You have to phone your sister.
Vado **a** casa di Giorgio con gli altri amici.	I'm going to George's house with some friends.

The **perfect tenses** are formed:

• with the auxiliary verb **essere** (to be) – for verbs of movement and other intransitive verbs – plus the **past participle** which must agree with the subject.

È arrivata/Sono arrivati alle sette.	She arrived/They arrived at seven.
Sei riuscito/riuscita?	Did you manage?

• or with the auxiliary verb **avere** (to have) – for transitive verbs – plus the **past participle** which is invariable.

Abbiamo già **mangiato** un panino.	We've already had a sandwich.
Non **ho capito** questa regola.	I haven't understood this rule.

• The **passive tense** is formed with the verb **essere** (to be) and the **past participle** which must agree with the subject.

Sono stato assunto da una grossa azienda.	I've been taken on by a large company.
Questa casa **fu costruita** da mio zio.	This house was built by my uncle.

• There are many **reflexive verbs** in Italian and these are formed using the reflexive pronouns *mi*, *ti*, *si*, *ci*, *vi* and the auxiliary verb **essere** (to be). Verbs requiring a reflexive pronoun are fairly uncommon in English; a form using **get** is usually preferred (e.g. I got dressed).

Io mi sono lavato	I got washed
Tu ti sei lavato	You got washed
Egli si è lavato/Lei si è lavata	He/She got washed
Noi ci siamo lavati	We got washed
Voi vi siete lavati	You got washed
Essi si sono lavati/ Esse si sono lavate	They (m./f.) got washed

• Choosing the correct tense to use is quite complex in Italian so it is better – at least in the beginning – to stick to the simplest forms possible. Be careful, however, when using the conjunction **se** (if) as this is followed by a subjunctive in Italian.

Se potessi, verrei.	I would come if I could.
Se me **l'avesse detto**, lo avrei aiutato.	If (s)he had told me, I would have helped her/him.

A. Auxiliary verbs

The auxiliary verbs in Italian are *essere* (**to be**) and *avere* (**to have**). They are both irregular verbs so you need to be careful when you conjugate them.

ESSERE	**AVERE**
TO BE	TO HAVE

Indicativo presente/Simple present

Io sono/I am	Io ho/I have
Tu sei	Tu hai
Egli è	Egli ha
Noi siamo	Noi abbiamo
Voi siete	Voi avete
Essi sono	Essi hanno

Indicativo imperfetto/Imperfect or past descriptive

Io ero/I was	Io avevo/I had
Tu eri	Tu avevi
Egli era	Egli aveva
Noi eravamo	Noi avevamo
Voi eravate	Voi avevate
Essi erano	Essi avevano

Indicativo passato prossimo/Present perfect

Io sono stato/I have been	Io ho avuto/I have had
Tu sei stato	Tu hai avuto
Egli è stato	Egli ha avuto
Noi siamo stati	Noi abbiamo avuto
Voi siete stati	Voi avete avuto
Essi sono stati	Essi hanno avuto

Indicativo futuro/Future

Io sarò/I will be
Tu sarai
Egli sarà
Noi saremo
Voi sarete
Essi saranno

Io avrò/I will have
Tu avrai
Egli avrà
Noi avremo
Voi avrete
Essi avranno

Imperativo/Imperative

Sii/Be
Siamo
Siate

Abbi/Have
Abbiamo
Abbiate

Congiuntivo presente/Present subjunctive

Che io sia*
Che tu sia
Che egli sia
Che noi siamo
Che voi siate
Che essi siano

Che io abbia
Che tu abbia
Che egli abbia
Che noi abbiamo
Che voi abbiate
Che essi abbiano

* Rarely used in English.

Condizionale presente/Conditional (simple)

Io sarei/I would be
Tu saresti
Egli sarebbe
Noi saremmo
Voi sareste
Essi sarebbero

Io avrei/I would have
Tu avresti
Egli avrebbe
Noi avremmo
Voi avreste
Essi avrebbero

Participio passato/Past participle

Stato/Been

Avuto/Had

Gerundio/Gerund

Essendo/Being

Avendo/Having

B. Regular verbs

There are three groups, or conjugations, of regular Italian verbs. The infinitives consist of a stem followed by the endings **-are** (*parlare*), **-ere** (*temere*) and **-ire** (*partire*). The main forms of these regular verbs are given below.

Present	Imperfect	Future	Imperative	Past participle

Parlare   To speak

Present	Imperfect	Future	Imperative	Past participle
Io parlo	parlavo	parlerò		parlato
Tu parli	parlavi	parlerai	parla	
Egli parla	parlava	parlerà		
Noi parliamo	parlavamo	parleremo	parliamo	
Voi parlate	parlavate	parlerete	parlate	
Essi parlano	parlavano	parleranno		

Temere   To fear

Io temo	temevo	temerò		temuto
Tu temi	temevi	temerai	temi	
Egli teme	temeva	temerà		
Noi temiamo	temevamo	temeremo	temiamo	
Voi temete	temevate	temerete	temete	
Essi temono	temevano	temeranno		

Partire   To leave

Io parto	partivo	partirò		partito
Tu parti	partivi	partirai	parti	
Egli parte	partiva	partirà		
Noi partiamo	partivamo	partiremo	partiamo	
Voi partite	partivate	partirete	partite	
Essi partono	partivano	partiranno		

C. Irregular verbs

Irregular verbs (those which are not conjugated as in the above examples) are very common in Italian. Some of the most frequently used are given below.

Present	Imperfect	Future	Imperative	Past participle

Andare   To go

Present	Imperfect	Future	Imperative	Past participle
Io vado	andavo	andrò		andato
Tu vai	andavi	andrai	vai/va'	
Egli va	andava	andrà		
Noi andiamo	andavamo	andremo	andiamo	
Voi andate	andavate	andrete	andate	
Essi vanno	andavano	andranno		

Dare   To give

Present	Imperfect	Future	Imperative	Past participle
Io do	davo	darò		dato
Tu dai	davi	darai	dai/da'/dà	
Egli dà	dava	darà		
Noi diamo	davamo	daremo	diamo	
Voi date	davate	darete	date	
Essi danno	davano	daranno		

Dire   To say

Present	Imperfect	Future	Imperative	Past participle
Io dico	dicevo	dirò		detto
Tu dici	dicevi	dirai	dì	
Egli dice	diceva	dirà		
Noi diciamo	dicevamo	diremo	diciamo	
Voi dite	dicevate	direte	dite	
Essi dicono	dicevano	diranno		

Dovere   To have to

Present	Imperfect	Future	Imperative	Past participle
Io devo	dovevo	dovrò		dovuto
Tu devi	dovevi	dovrai	–	
Egli deve	doveva	dovrà		
Noi dobbiamo	dovevamo	dovremo	–	
Voi dovete	dovevate	dovrete	–	
Essi devono	dovevano	dovranno		

Fare   To do/make

Present	Imperfect	Future	Imperative	Past participle
Io faccio	facevo	farò		fatto
Tu fai	facevi	farai	fai/fa/fa'	
Egli fa	faceva	farà		
Noi facciamo	facevamo	faremo	facciamo	
Voi fate	facevate	farete	fate	
Essi fanno	facevano	faranno		

Present	Imperfect	Future	Imperative	Past participle

Potere To be able

Io posso	potevo	potrò		potuto
Tu puoi	potevi	potrai	–	
Egli può	poteva	potrà		
Noi possiamo	potevamo	potremo	–	
Voi potete	potevate	potrete	–	
Essi possono	potevano	potranno		

Venire To come

Io vengo	venivo	verrò		venuto
Tu vieni	venivi	verrai	vieni	
Egli viene	veniva	verrà		
Noi veniamo	venivamo	verremo	veniamo	
Voi venite	venivate	verrete	venite	
Essi vengono	venivano	verranno		

Volere To want

Io voglio	volevo	vorrò		voluto
Tu vuoi	volevi	vorrai	–	
Egli vuole	voleva	vorrà		
Noi vogliamo	volevamo	vorremo	–	
Voi volete	volevate	vorrete	–	
Essi vogliono	volevano	vorranno		

Finito di stampare nel maggio 2000
dalle Industrie per le Arti Grafiche Garzanti-Verga s.r.l.
Cernusco sul Naviglio (Mi)